Teaching and Learning
and the Curriculum

Also available from Continuum

Teaching and Learning and the Curriculum

A Critical Introduction

**Emmanuel Mufti and
Mark Peace**

continuum

Continuum International Publishing Group

The Tower Building   80 Maiden Lane
11 York Road   Suite 704
London SE1 7NX   New York NY 10038

www.continuumbooks.com

British Library Cataloguing-in-Publication Data
A catalogue record for this book is available from the British Library.

ISBN: 978-1-4411-5484-2 hardcover
        978-1-4411-4351-8 paperback

Library of Congress Cataloging-in-Publication Data
Mufti, Emmanuel.
 Teaching and learning and the curriculum: a critical introduction /
Emmanuel Mufti and Mark Peace.
   p. cm.
 Includes bibliographical references and index.
   ISBN 978-1-4411-5484-2 (hardcover) – ISBN 978-1-4411-4351-8 (pbk.)
1. Education–Curricula–Social aspects.   2. Critical pedagogy.   3. Learning.
4. Constructivism (Education)   I. Peace, Mark. II. Title.
LB1570.M77 2012
370.11'5–dc23
                                                    2011023010

Typeset by Newgen Imaging Systems Pvt Ltd, Chennai, India
Printed and bound in India

This book is dedicated to
Helen, Sarah, Rashida, Samuel and Emily

Contents

Introduction

Education is a contested enterprise. That its purposes – who succeeds and who does not, which qualifications count for more than others and whose ideas are given preference – are all issues subject to debate and challenge is not surprising, as all of society has a large stake in the educational system. Virtually anyone may currently be directly involved as teacher, parent, pupil or student, either studying education or indeed any other subject. Even those not within one of these groups in the present well have been in the past; furthermore, given the way in which education operates, what it means to be educated and what type of individual and society the system creates is of interest to us all.

A casual perusal of any newspaper will confirm the importance of education. A feature article may be one directly concerning schools, colleges or universities, or it may have a more general focus: on the economy, communities, youth behaviour, obesity, issues of respect or new directions in technology

---

Stop, Think, Do

Ask people around you what responsibility schools have. Should they focus only on academic achievement, or should our schools help individuals develop in a variety of ways?

Search newspaper websites for information on education. What is their focus?

Should schools be concerned with issues such as those above? Is it practical to expect them to?

The fact remains that education impacts all aspects of all individuals' lives, as well as the ways in which society operates at all levels: locally, nationally and, increasingly, internationally. This impact is felt in terms of how able people are to access jobs both now and in the future; of how competitive the country is internationally with regard to possessing highly skilled, highly educated individuals; of how people make sense of information they receive; and of the views they hold about each other.

Two things are clear then: that education is of paramount importance and that at the heart of the educational process are the schools and, most importantly, the teachers and learners within them.

Placing teachers and learners where they belong – at the heart of the education process – this volume's chapters examine the ways people learn and the ways in which the relationship between schools, teachers and pupils is made manifest. However, that is not to say that this is a simple, uncomplicated relationship. Education, including all those who work and study within it, is subject to various controls and pressures. Some of them we have briefly mentioned above; their drivers tend to be the media and the public. Other pressures come more directly from those ultimately in charge of the educational process in this country: those in the government in office at a given time.

The level of control in education is interesting, as there is no one system of teaching and learning with which all those involved would agree. When attempting to create an overall approach, politicians and educators often discover that evidence can be contradictory and challenging. Whether one is talking about the entire system of education, with its various schools and its national curriculum, or is discussing how best to get a particular child to read or learn about and understand a relevant issue, there are myriad alternatives to navigate. Some approaches will derive from educators with much practical experience of the process; others may stem from academics who seek to examine the system from a slightly more removed point of view; yet others, deriving from politicians, company directors, the media or the general public, may come with their own agendas and with ideas about how best to realize them.

So what are the implications for those working or studying within education? That it is pointless trying to navigate through these often conflicting theories, opinions and agendas? That it is better to accept the status quo and accept uncritically the information that is presented in the loudest format? Hopefully not. This volume does not attempt to tell them how to teach or how – or indeed for what purpose – they should learn; rather it presents a range of issues for them to digest and be challenged by, so that they can form their own directions, approaches and opinions. What the volume says is this: whether you are currently teaching or hope to be in the near future, your role is an extremely important one. If you are in any doubt about that, just check how much influence is being brought to bear on the educational process. Teachers and educators are in the best position to understand the process, but they need to examine a range of approaches, to subject theory to critical analysis, in order to make sense of both the overall system and the more specific context they find yourself in. We hope that this volume can aid them in doing that.

This volume covers a range of areas: those related to the system generally, to teachers within it, to the subjects and curricula they operate within, to the aims of central governments and to the implications of these aims. This content, or indeed any content encountered, should not be accepted uncritically; readers should consider its uses and implications and seek to create their own interpretations.

In Chapter 1, we examine traditional learning theories; most notably, those that fall under two main headings – behaviourism and constructivism. The former, with notable theorists such as Pavlov, Skinner and Bandura, focuses upon the ways behaviour is learned, what is acceptable and what is not, and also upon the ways in which that behaviour can influence one to understand what knowledge is most important. The examination of constructivism, which introduces the ideas of Piaget and Vygotsky, discusses the ways in which an individual makes sense of knowledge and how it links to prior knowledge, challenging conceptions of an issue and often making people rethink and reformulate existing conceptions.

Chapter 2 has a similar focus but moves on from the more traditional and well-known theorists to those who have followed in their footsteps and, in further developing traditional perspectives, provided more opportunities to challenge and develop the understanding of the learning process. These theorists challenge the concept of learning itself; they question whether people confuse learning with what takes place in the classroom rather than consider the range of ways and places in which individuals learn.

Chapter 3 asks us that the concept of intelligence, most notably its use and misuse in separating individuals along educational lines, be critically considered. It goes on to discuss the concept of learning preferences and how learners best assimilate and retain information – for example, whether people like to experience issues practically and understand their implications or whether they are happy dealing with them in a more theoretical manner. This chapter calls for an understanding that both intelligence and learning preferences or styles are socially constructed by examining their historical development. That is not to say that there are no important issues within education – quite the contrary – it simply reiterates the importance of a critical and enquiring approach to these theoretical perspectives.

Chapter 4 moves away from learners and addresses the concept of curriculum. It begins by examining the historical traditions of the curriculum and the way in which people view the world. It then examines three traditional approaches: liberal, instrumental and critical. It questions how 'natural' the curriculum is and how much it is influenced by and in turn influences the society it exists within.

Chapter 5 examines how education in all its aspects – curriculum, exams, even the training and direction of teachers and schools – has been subject to increasingly centralized control. The chapter demonstrates that centralized control is not a given and is in fact a relatively recent introduction. It questions the purpose and the implications of this control and asks the reader to consider its ideological basis.

Chapter 6 makes a start at appreciating the fundamental challenges of the education system. Too often, as the chapter demonstrates, who the winners and losers are is based on social class, ethnicity and gender. The chapter explores how outcomes are often considered unchangeable and natural and suggests ways that individuals and groups can resist and challenge the system. Working in conjunction with Chapter 9, it asks whether the individual should change to meet the requirements of the system or whether it is the system that is at fault.

Chapter 7 examines the role of technology from both historical and contemporary points of view, starting with the greater availability of knowledge thanks to the printing press and other innovations and the implications of a much wider segment of society having access to that knowledge. Will Wikis and similar tools broaden individuals' capacity to access and, perhaps more importantly, create knowledge? The chapter also explores the ever-widening possibilities for learning outside the classroom and sees challenges to the existing knowledge base from new technologies as again demonstrating how education is constantly changing.

Chapter 8 examines the roles played by teachers and the school ethos. Teaching styles and culture are explored, as are the questions of what it is that makes a good teacher and whether teaching is being deprofessionalized. The chapter also considers the implications of focusing primarily on the practice of teaching rather than allowing teachers the opportunity to reflect and review the theory that supports them.

Finally, we reiterate that it is the teacher's role as an educator which is of paramount importance; teachers should be free to form their own understanding of that role. Theories and controversies surrounding education should be seen as an opportunity for teachers to navigate their own path.

1 Learning Theories: Conventions and Traditions

Chapter Outline

The central content of this text is structured around the division between two core concepts in education studies: pedagogy and curriculum. In this chapter and the two that follow, our focus is very much on the former of these concepts: on the techniques and approaches which educators use to promote learning and, more fundamentally, on the philosophies and theories which underpin these practices. We begin to explore what the nature and processes of 'learning' actually mean in theoretical terms by focusing on the two 'conventional' approaches which comprise the foundations and bedrock of learning theory: behaviourism and constructivism (or cognitive psychology).

Following a common structure, consideration of each of these approaches begins by exploring the most important central features of the perspective before providing a summary of its history, development and key contributing theorists. The final segment of each exploration is given over to a critical examination of the influences and legacies of the perspectives which considers the implications of theories for pedagogy and policy and the tensions and problems inherent to these influences.

Stop, Think, Do

Think of an experience of your own in which learning has been really effective. Analyse your experience. What were the features that made it effective? What does the experience tell about the process of learning in general?

Behaviourism

It is fitting for two key reasons to begin this exploration of the nature of learning with the behavioural school. First, in dating back to the early 1900s, it is the older of the conventional approaches to learning. Secondly, its principles and implications are perhaps more easily compartmentalized and understood. The approach, in parallel with the later development of constructivism, emerged from simultaneous though unconnected work in the Western world and Russia. Within these regions a number of founding theorists, working independently, were committed to a core philosophy, one most famously expressed by the American theorist John Watson:

> Psychology as the behaviorist views it is a purely objective experimental branch of natural science. . . . [I]ntrospection forms no essential part of its methods, nor is the scientific value of its data dependent upon the readiness with which they lend themselves to interpretation. . . . [T]he behaviorist, in his efforts to get a unitary scheme of animal response, recognizes no dividing line between man and brute. (Watson, 1914)

Central to the behavioural approach, then, is the assertion that we should seek to understand learning in the same terms of reference as a scientist might – most importantly, through seeking direct, observable (or empirical) evidence. In turn, this commitment suggests that learning – indeed all activity – should be understood in a way which avoids the guesswork involved in hypothesizing about what goes on inside people's heads (what Watson refers to in the above quote as 'introspection'), a process commonly associated with popular representations of psychology. Instead, we should focus only on those phenomena that we can *observe*: individuals' external interactions with the environment – their 'behaviours'.

This basic principle, then, sets out the remit of behavioural psychology: the notion that the 'behaviour' is the basic unit of analysis and, thus, that learning should be considered to comprise an array of acquired behaviours. Understanding how any of these behaviours arises and stabilizes necessitates an interrogation of the external conditions which surround it: the things that happened in the run-up to its occurring (its antecedents) and those that happened afterwards (its consequences). This framework of analysis, according to behaviourists, can be applied universally to all behaviours, in humans and animals alike. As such, a common feature of behavioural research is the study of animals in order to extrapolate understandings about human learning.

Classical conditioning: Learning and instinct

One of the most famous studies in this mode of enquiry – and one of the most important early contributions to the behavioural perspective – is to be found in the work of the Russian physiologist Ivan Pavlov (1927). Originally examining digestion, Pavlov had been collecting dogs' saliva (normally produced instinctively by an animal in order to aid the breakdown of food) to examine its function. Pavlov noted, however, that the dogs he was studying had begun to salivate in response to other incidental stimuli, such as a light being switched on. Pavlov hypothesized that the dogs he had been studying had begun to associate the stimuli which had presented with the food with the food itself; thus, a seemingly random stimulus now elicited a previously instinctive response. To test this hypothesis, Pavlov repeatedly presented food to the dogs while at the same time ringing a bell. Eventually, the animals began to salivate without any food being presented.

The experiment supported Pavlov's hypothesis; he consequently developed the notion of **classical conditioning** to explain the phenomenon. He argued that if a neutral stimulus is repeatedly paired with an unconditioned stimulus, the two become associated. The result of this is that the neutral stimulus becomes a conditioned stimulus, able to invoke the previously instinctive (and now conditioned) response. Pavlov argued that, ultimately, even the most complicated behaviour can be explained as complex webs and chains of classical conditioning.

The problem facing these conclusions is, of course, the questionable applicability of applying findings from the study of animals – which are incapable of higher-level cognitive processes – to humans. However, in a now infamous experimental case study, John Watson and Rosalie Rayner (1920) demonstrated that these processes are indeed applicable to human subjects. The study itself is subject to extensive misrepresentation and misinterpretation (see Harris, 1979, for a fuller critique). The essence of the study, however, holds that the researchers applied the principles of classical conditioning to a young child, named Little Albert, in order to produce a phobia in the child. In order to do so, they repeatedly presented Albert with a pet white rat, accompanied by a loud noise generated by banging a hammer on a metal bar behind the child's head. Eventually, the researchers found that they could produce the fear response simply by presenting the child with the rat, without the accompanying bang. This fear began to fade as time went on; however, the association could be renewed by repeating the original procedure a few times. Watson and Rayner also found that Albert developed phobias of objects, such as white cotton wool, which shared characteristics with the rat.

Watson and Rayner's study supports the view that classical conditioning is a genuine feature of human as well as animal learning. It also demonstrates two additional concepts originally outlined by Pavlov. First, that while a conditioned association can be incredibly strong, it begins to fade, if not reinforced, until it disappears completely (a process called **extinction**). Second, the study suggests that associations can broaden beyond a specific stimulus (called **generalization**); so, for instance, a child bullied in class can rapidly develop a more generalized phobia of school.

Operant conditioning: Learning and intentional action

The early work of Pavlov and Watson shares a focus on impulsive and instinctive behaviour and on the ways in which these knee-jerk responses can be learned through association. Such an approach is useful when examining how organisms react to stimuli, but it is, however, much less effective when considering more complex intentional (or operant) behaviour – when, that is, an organism voluntarily interacts with its environment. It is to this focus that behaviourist thinkers of the second wave turned their attention.

Early explanations of the learning of operant behaviour can be found in the work of the American psychologist Edward Thorndike (1911), which aimed to understand complex voluntary behaviour in animals by placing cats in mazes and recording the learning curve which led to their escape. On the basis of these controlled observations, Thorndike concluded that all learning occurs through trial and error but that particular conditions (or 'laws') guide this experimentation so that it is not entirely haphazard.

- **Law of Readiness**: learning occurs best when it taps into the organism's particular goals or needs. Thus, it can only ever be counterproductive to attempt to encourage behaviour when it does not suit the needs of the organism.
- **Law of Exercise**: learning occurs through repetition and practice, and forgetting occurs when this is not present.
- **Law of Recency**: organisms tend to fall back on more recent experiences to reach goals rather than older ones.
- **Law of Effect**: the outcome of a behaviour impacts on the likelihood of its being repeated. Thus, behaviours which are rewarded are more likely to reoccur than those which are punished.

In this early work, Thorndike therefore begins to explain some of the processes by which more complex operant behaviours are learned and shaped. It is, however, the work of B. F. Skinner, extending on these foundations, which most famously established these learning principles. In particular, Skinner (1938; 1953; 1988) extends Thorndike's Law of Effect by exploring the variety of different consequences that might follow behaviour and the dynamics involved in its repetition. As a result, Skinner identifies four different forms of outcome (the **Operant Quadrant**):

- **Positive Reinforcement**: a direct pleasant outcome following a behaviour. In a classroom, this might be praise or a treat.
- **Positive Punishment**: a direct unpleasant outcome following a particular behaviour. A teacher might, for instance, shout at a student.

- **Negative Reinforcement**: the removal of an unpleasant situation when a particular behaviour is performed, thus producing a sense of relief. In a school context, a teacher might make a certain student feel under pressure until she gives an answer or admission.
- **Negative Punishment**: involves taking away a reward or removing a pleasant situation. An illustration might be the common use of detention in schools.

It is worth clarifying here the use of the terms *positive* and *negative* in Skinner's typology. They are used in the mathematical sense rather than to indicate 'good' and 'bad'. Thus, positive outcomes are where something (be it a reward or a punishment) is given to the individual, while negative outcomes involve taking something away. In addition, Skinner distinguished between primary and generalized outcomes. **Primary outcomes** work because they appeal to instincts or drives (such as pleasure and pain), while **generalized outcomes** work because the individual has learned to associate them with primary outcomes (e.g. verbal praise) through a process of classical conditioning.

Skinner (1947) devised an apparatus to test the impacts of these outcomes in carefully controlled ways. It consisted of a pigeon cage which was capable of delivering reinforcements and punishments in the form of food pellets and electric shocks. Through the use of this apparatus, Skinner was able to demonstrate how complex behaviours can be gradually shaped through a process of successive approximation by shifting the criteria on which rewards are delivered (the **reinforcement contingencies**) until the desired behaviour is achieved. Skinner (1957) argues that it is exactly through this form of shaping that we learn a complex skill such as language, in which informal reinforcements from parents (such as fuss and attention) shape babbling and cooing into verbalizations akin to everyday language.

The emphasis on rewards in shaping behaviour is intentional. Skinner's research suggests that such an outcome is much more effective than punishment. Where reinforcement encourages a very definite behaviour, punishment only discourages unwanted ones without a clear pattern to displace them. Haphazard use of punishments, then, can lead to a sense of bewilderment and confusion – a process known as the formation of **learned helplessness** (Seligman and Maier, 1967). Further, punishment can be a blunt instrument, discouraging desirable behaviours as well as unwanted ones. Admonishing an incorrect answer in class, for instance, discourages not only the answer itself but also the act of volunteering an answer.

A final facet of Skinner's work concerns the quantity and rhythm (rather than the quality) of particular outcomes. As such, a strand of his research and writing concerns **schedules of reinforcement** (1957; 1969) and explores the impacts made when the frequency of rewards is varied. He explores three distinct forms of schedule:

- **Continuous reinforcement**, which occurs every time a particular behaviour occurs.
- **Interval reinforcement**, which is given after fixed occurrences of the behaviour but not every time.
- **Variable reinforcement**, which is given randomly, though always after the desired behaviour.

In exploring these schedules, Skinner examined their impact on both acquisition and extinction of the desired behaviour. He found that under continuous reinforcement, the behaviour would be learned quickly but would also fade quickly once rewards were withheld. Under variable reinforcement, in contrast, behaviours took much longer to form but were then much more stable once the rewards were removed. Interval reinforcement produced acquisition and extinction rates somewhere in between.

Observational learning

Each of the behavioural approaches so far places emphasis on the primacy of individual experience, in that persons themselves must exhibit a behaviour and receive an outcome in order for learning processes to occur. A final (and later) branch of behavioural psychology, broadly known as **social learning theory**, stands at odds with this assertion. Instead, this approach notes that an important source of learning occurs through the observation of others. We should note that, in taking this approach, social learning theory begins to deviate from the strict precepts of behavioural psychology as established by Watson, in that it hypothesizes about internal mental processes, which are not empirically observable. This said, however, the approach does still set out to understand observational learning in as scientific a framework as possible.

Perhaps the most famous proponent of social learning theory is Albert Bandura (1977) – though his arguments owe much to an already established tradition (Miller and Dollard, 1941; Rotter, 1945). Bandura's key argument is that particular behavioural patterns can be acquired by an individual simply through watching other people perform them; he calls these demonstrations **models**. Equally, the processes of reward and punishment observed in others (**vicarious outcomes**) can impact on the likelihood that particular behaviours will be imitated and repeated by the observer. Most famously, Bandura (1973) has used this as the framework for the explanation of aggressive behaviour, though there is also a range of more mundane applications. Teachers might, for instance, punish particular behaviours in order to set an example or make a fuss over good work in order to raise aspirations in a group as a whole.

Stop, Think, Do

Think about the ways in which each of the principles of conditioning explored so far might be applied to a classroom setting. Reflect on the reasons why some people might see the use of behaviourist tactics on classroom practice as limited in effectiveness – or even unethical.

Influence, legacies and controversies

The behavioural perspective on learning has had (and continues to have) a wide-ranging and subtle influence on classroom practice. Most notably, the approach has become closely associated with strategies of classroom management, wherein systems of rewards and punishments are seen to be crucial tools in shaping and moulding behaviour into acceptable patterns. Often these principles are used informally and instinctively; in actual day-to-day practice, teachers rarely make recourse to underlying theory. This fact reflects the extent to which the approaches have been successful in gaining status as 'common sense'. One common manifestation is the use of sticker charts, on which children can record rewards and reinforcements – a strategy technically referred to as a **token economy**.

While the application of behavioural techniques to classroom management is pervasive – and many teachers would cite the usefulness of their application – it is important to recognize that there are a number of important problems with them. Indeed, the extent to which the techniques are perceived as commonsensical increases the necessity to view them through a critical lens. A number of criticisms stem from the theoretical basis of behaviourism itself: from the view that individuals can be programmed to behave in particular ways through the application of rewards and punishments. Most fundamentally, humanist theorists take exception to the motivation of this stance, arguing that its appeal to the 'power motive' – the impulse to control and shape children – is unethical. Further, the approach is intentionally blind to children's beliefs and cognitions, to the thinking which lies behind actions deemed 'bad behaviour'. Thus, some critics argue that a blind application of behavioural classroom-management techniques is only ever effective as a half measure. Such an approach may discourage poor behaviour and encourage good behaviour – but not the underlying understandings of why particular behaviours are good and bad. As a consequence, the application of rewards and punishments, without accompanying cognitive scaffolding, misses the opportunity to help learners develop their own moral reasoning. In turn, this means that they are less able to self-regulate behaviour when the context surrounding it shifts.

A second theme in the critique of behavioural strategies for classroom management focuses on the mythology it constructs around 'bad behaviour', which it tends to view as internal to children themselves. As such, it can be blind to the contextual factors which contribute to that behaviour, whether out of school or more immediately in the classroom. In addition, teachers can find themselves tempted by the allure of rewards and punishments as an easy fix to a 'badly behaved' class, when an enquiry into how interesting or relevant lessons are may be a more effective strategy.

Finally, the use of behavioural classroom-management strategies is controversial in the messages that children are sent about the motivations for learning; which, it is implied, is engaged with in order to achieve rewards or avoid punishments. The latter of these is obviously problematic – no educator wants students to learn purely out of fear – but there are also subtle problems with the use of rewards, problems that merit investigation. Forms of extrinsic (i.e., external to the person) motivation can easily overpower the more valuable possibility of intrinsic motivation: that children might want to learn because the act of learning and understanding the world is valuable in and of itself.

A range of theoretical and empirical work has established the problematic nature of overuse of rewards as a motivating process. In Marxist sociology, for instance, the argument has been made that such an application works to prepare children for lives in meaningless and unrewarding careers in which the key source of motivation is the pay check at the end of the month rather than enjoyment of the job (Bowles and Gintis, 1976). Elsewhere, a number of pieces of research in psychology have noted the problem of **overjustification** – that the use of extrinsic motivators can actively harm intrinsic motivation (Greene et al., 1976; Lepper et al., 1973). In simple terms, the principle here is that individuals gradually learn to do things that they may otherwise do out of enjoyment or interest only because a reward is expected. Thus, when that reward is not forthcoming, the individual loses interest in the activity. The fundamental implication of this form of argument and research is not to assume that the use of rewards is an automatically positive feature of a classroom environment and learning experience.

The influence of behaviourism in classroom management is, then, perhaps the approach's most notable legacy. It has, however, also found influence in the actual teaching of subject content. Historically, this was more immediately perceptible: in the use, for instance, of rote learning through repetition (a strategy which alludes to Thorndike's Law of Exercise). The notion of modelling (as described by Bandura) has also been influential, notably in the teaching of practical and vocational subjects, in which demonstration is paramount, but also in more traditionally academic pursuits. Teachers, for instance, model handwriting to young children – and provide 'model answers' to older ones – on the assumption that imitation will lead to an improvement in their own work.

There have also been attempts to systematize behavioural psychology in the teaching of subject content – work which began with Skinner's proposals (1958) for **programmed learning** (or programmed instruction). Here, learners are given snippets of information, ordered logically, followed by a comprehension question. If the question is answered correctly, a reward is administered (perhaps simply in the form of praise);

if the question is answered incorrectly, some additional corrective information is provided before taking the learner back to the previous step. More sophisticated systems of programmed instruction might 'branch' content so as to provide different pacing for students of differing ability – for instance, more steps to completing a sequence of learning might be provided for less able pupils. Here, Skinner envisaged children working independently on packages of learning contained in specially designed textbooks, or 'learning machines', which provided information, received feedback and administered outcomes.

Such an approach has never garnered significant mainstream use in education, but the recent popularization of the internet in education, and the rise of virtual learning environments (VLEs) has prompted resurgence in the use of programmed learning and instruction. On one hand, the principles of feedback and correction can be found in the prevalent use of quizzes in such environments, but they are also more broadly embedded in the information-task process which often underpins them (e.g. delivering 'content' through a podcast and then asking students to engage in an individual or group follow-up task). We should note that this is not the only philosophy underpinning the use of online spaces; alternative paradigms are discussed in both Chapter 2 and Chapter 7, 'Knowledge and Technology'.

As already noted, behavioural approaches have not established the same level of influence in teaching and learning as they have in classroom management, where the criticisms of the perspective are more apparent. Most notably, the emphasis on repetition and the 'performance' of right answers and on the refusal to engage with internal cognitive features of the learner tends to promote only a surface understanding. Thus, students are able to produce the correct answers they have been trained to recite (in parrot fashion), but they have no deep understanding of the significance of these answers, nor of their links to other aspects of the students' learning. For this reason, detractors argue that behavioural learning strategies are weak equally in the learners' retention of understanding and in sophistication, particularly in the ability to synthesize – to make links across distinct areas of knowledge.

In response to these problems, some theorists therefore reject the behavioural tenet of ignoring unobservable processes within the minds of learners. Instead, they maintain that learning is fundamentally embedded in these processes, and ignoring them therefore offers a poor insight and promotes a low standard of understanding. It is to these theorists to whom we now turn our attention.

Constructivism

A crucial tenet in the behavioural approach to learning is, then, a focus on external observable behaviours and the contexts which surround them, actively avoiding guesswork about the individuals' internal mental states and processes. Other perspectives are, however, deeply critical of this stance. They highlight that learning is a fundamentally internal phenomenon, governed by processes and structures inside individuals' minds. Thus, any approach which ignores cognitive functioning can offer only a limited and surface insight, one akin to an attempt to understand the workings of a clock by watching its movement without exploring its internal mechanisms.

One of the most important outcomes of a focal shift to internal mental (or cognitive) processes has been the evolution of **constructivism**, a perspective so called because it maintains that learning is an active process by which individuals construct and develop their own understandings of the world based on their experiences. This contrasts with a more transmissive approach to learning, which might see 'understanding' as something which is transferred directly from teacher to student.

Schemata and the Western tradition

A core concept of the constructivist approach to learning is that of **schema** – a mental structure through which we organize our understandings and expectations of the world through hierarchies of properties (think of a tree diagram). It is these schemata which allow us, for instance, to distinguish between horses and cows by looking for key characteristics. On a more sophisticated level, schemata allow us to interpret geographical features, understand complex mathematical formulae and understand acceptable behaviour associated with particular roles and contexts. The notion that we have mental 'maps' which organize our perceptions and expectations has a long history; it is found, for instance, in Plato's theory of forms (2007), and nomenclature as 'schema' is found in the work of the eighteenth-century philosopher Immanuel Kant (2007). It was with the work of the Swiss psychologist Jean Piaget (1971), however, that, the concept entered mainstream educational theory with the assertion that all learning involves the creation and refinement of schemata.

Piaget argues that as we grow and mature, our schemata become increasingly complex and intricate; allowing us access to more sophisticated understandings and interpretations of the world. A baby, for instance, has only its instincts through which to interpret and interact with its environment. As that baby grows, however, these instincts will quickly become refined and replaced with constructed schemata. It will begin to 'carve' the world into categories, beginning with the crucial distinction between self and environment and then distinguishing other external stimuli: people from objects, parents from strangers and so on. As it develops further, the child will develop the schemata necessary to deal with more abstract and symbolic concepts, such as spoken (later, written) language – together with mathematical and logical reasoning.

Underpinning this process of refinement is, according to Piaget (1985), the innate urge to maintain cognitive **equilibrium**, a state of balance between internal schemata and external environment; in other words, the ability to fully and properly understand what is going on around us using our existing cognitive maps. Crucially, however, Piaget argues that on occasion environmental information doesn't match neatly with existing schemata, causing a state of **disequilibrium**. It is in this context that existing schemata must be revised and modified in order to bring expectation and experience into balance – through which learning occurs.

In practice, Piaget argues that two **adaptation strategies** are involved in modifying schemata. **Assimilation** is the process by which new information is added to an existing schema, without altering it in major way (a case of 'filling in the details'). For instance, a child may have read a picture book with her parents and developed a schema which allows her to recognize a dog by its ears, four legs and tail. However, if that child were to encounter a real dog in the park, she would be bombarded with new information which her schema does not prepare her to expect; the dog might bark and bound up to her; it might be furry and a bit smelly. This new information will throw the child into a state of disequilibrium;

her mental schema and her environment would not match exactly. Consequently, in order to bring about balance, the child would have to incorporate (or assimilate) this new information into her existing schema framework.

On other occasions, we encounter environmental stimuli which require more radical restructuring of schemata – the removal of misconceptions and creation of entirely new categories, for instance. Piaget calls this **accommodation**. Our fictional child, for instance, might encounter a new animal, one with many of the characteristics needed for it to match the dog schema: four legs, ears, fur. However, it might also have characteristics which contradict the schema; it might miaow rather than bark. Once again, this new information will cause a state of disequilibrium; in order to bring about balance, a new 'cat' schema must be created to allow the child to distinguish between dogs and this strange new animal.

Consequently, as a person grows and learns more about his or her world, the schemata become more specialized and refined until they are able to perform complex abstract cognitions. It is important to note, however, that – according to Piaget (1971) – the refinement of schemata does not occur without restrictions. At different ages, we are capable of performing different types of cognitive processes, and the extent of our schemata is consequently limited by biological boundaries. As a result, the reason why six-year-old rocket scientists are few and far between is that the cognitive differences between children and adults are qualitative as well as quantitative. In other words, development is governed not just by the amount of information absorbed by the individual, but also by the types of cognitive operations that can be performed on that information – that is, the way that we can transform and manipulate information in our minds. These operations are, in turn, determined by the child's age and the resultant physiological development.

Piaget consequently argues that as children age, they move through a series of stages, each of which brings with it the ability to perform increasingly sophisticated cognitive operations. In brief these are the following:

- **Sensorimotor stage** (birth to 2 years). Here the infant's only method of processing and interacting with their environment is physically, through senses and limbs.

Initially, this is done through reflexes, but these are gradually shaped into habits and then intentional motion, as the child gradually learns to distinguish self from environment and between objects in the child's universe of existence. Towards the end of the phase, the child begins to become interested in particular properties of objects (e.g. colour) and develop a sense of object permanence – the capacity to realize that objects still exist even when they are removed from sight.

- **Preoperational stage** (2 to 7 years). The child becomes increasingly curious about the surroundings and begins to develop the ability to represent objects symbolically together with the capacity to form stable concepts and perform basic reasoning. This is, however, limited; the child is unable to perform many operations. Egocentrism (the inability to understand other people's point of view), centration (a focus on one property of an object) and animism (the assumption of sentience in inanimate objects) are, for instance, common.

- **Concrete operational stage** (7 to 11 years). This phase of development brings with it the ability to undertake basic cognitive procedures: transforming concepts and ideas mentally. The child becomes less egocentric, and the tendency towards centration reduces. Seriation (the capacity to organize objects according to various properties) and reversibility (the understanding that an object, once changed, can be changed back to its original state) also develop.

- **Formal operational stage** (11 to 16 years). The key hallmark of the final stage of Piaget's model is a transition from concrete to abstract thinking; for instance, using symbolic mathematics. Here the ability to hypothesize and predict develops, overtaking the trial-and-error learning of prior phases, and the individual develops a much stronger capacity to conceptualize the future and to think imaginatively and ideologically.

Piaget therefore proposes a model of learning which might be imagined as governed by two layers. The first is the refinement of schemata through disequilibrium and the consequent processes of assimilation and accommodation. Beyond this, though, learning is governed by biological age, which sets constraints on how information can be processed by the learner.

Stop, Think, Do

Draw a flow chart to represent the ways in which a schema might distinguish four different types of animal. Consider the processes by which a toddler might construct this schema. Apply these ideas to a process of learning further along in life (e.g. distinguishing geographical features from each other).

The Soviet tradition

Piaget's model of learning and child development remains the dominant one in the foundations of Western thinking on learning. An important alternative approach was, however, proposed by the Russian psychologist Lev Vygotsky (1987; 1978). Vygotsky and Piaget are often presented as opposites, but in reality, the two thinkers have much in common. Fundamentally, they are both constructivists – in that they see knowledge as something that is actively accumulated and compiled by the individual – and they both have a place for schemata in their approaches.

Where the two thinkers differ is in their conceptualization of the mechanisms which guide and inhibit learning (the formation of schemata). Piaget's theory is structural, arguing that development is governed by physiological age-related stages. Vygotsky, by contrast, sees the culture and context in which the individual exists as much more important than biology. He maintains that 'culture' represents not only the accumulated knowledge of a society but also its means of intellectual adaptation – the mechanisms through which individuals within the culture transform and manipulate that knowledge. Thus, learning, for Vygotsky, is the gradual process by which this culture is internalized and, with it, both the content of knowledge and the tools by which that knowledge is transformed and manipulated.

Following a trend in Soviet thought (e.g. Bakhtin, 1982) and deeply influenced by Marxism, Vygotsky therefore sees thought as culturally mediated – emphasizing language as the medium through which this occurs. He observed, for instance, that children often self-narrate as they play but that this gradually diminishes over time. He argued that this represented a gradual mastery over the language needed to make sense of experiences until it is fully internalized and no longer needs to be vocally expressed. To return to the previous paragraph, learning the words by which a culture distinguishes different external phenomena (e.g. the ways in which different types of animals are distinguished) represents not only the 'content' of knowledge but also the deeper structure by which the world is classified. Thus, these words are tools to deploy in independent thinking.

A fundamental implication of Vygotsky's privileging of the social over the biological is that social interaction is crucial to learning. Without a cultural and communicative context, there is no way that children can ever learn – a point which contrasts with the Piagetian tendency to treat children as lone scientists. This, he argues, is true from the earliest forms of learning (such as the acquisition of language) and throughout educational experience. Interaction with others in this way allows learners to progress beyond what they could achieve in isolation, to bridge what Vygotsky calls the **zone of proximal development**.

Interaction alone, however, will not guarantee learning; Vygotsky goes some way to identifying the qualities necessary in those interactions in order for them to be effective. On one hand, there must be **subjectivity** involved; there must be differences in perception among participants. This might appear as a differing level of expertise or mastery, such as that found between teachers and students or between peers of different ability. It can be more subtle, though – for instance, in competing and contrasting opinions and perspectives on an issue. The crucial aspect here is not that one party has the 'right' answer, and another the 'wrong', but that there is space for disagreement and conflict from which new ideas and ways of thinking can be synthesized. Here Vygotsky draws on a Marxist tradition of dialectics.

The second crucial quality of an interaction, if it is to bridge the zone of proximal development, is the presence of **scaffolding**. Learners must be provided with frameworks and experiences which encourage them to extend their existing schemata and incorporate new skills competences and understandings. It is important to note that this is more than simply instruction; learning experiences must be presented in such a way as to actively challenge existing mental structures and provide frameworks for the formation of new ones. Equally, though, the most important form of scaffolding is found in day-to-day interactions – notably the ways in which teachers talk to learners. In asking a child to explain his or her thinking, for instance, a teacher helps the child to vocalize the language necessary to more fully understand the learning experiences. Similarly, the use of questioning to prompt thinking (traditionally called Socratic questioning) scaffolds language in such a way as to shift thinking in new directions.

Stop, Think, Do

Reflect on the ways group work has influenced your learning career. Try to explore some of the processes that made that group work successful. For instance, how did learning happen through the combination of different perspectives?

The second wave of constructivism

Piaget and Vygotsky could be held as two of the most important founding fathers of the cognitive approach – each working from a distinct theoretical starting point to expound some of the core principles governing the internal processes of learning. Other theorists have taken these ideas and applied them directly to the classroom setting, developing pedagogies (systems of learning and teaching) which draw on these ideas. These pedagogies all share a belief that learning is not a passive process, one in which the teacher imparts knowledge to students (a tendency in behavioural approaches). Rather, the learner is seen as an active agent, one who actively engages with and interprets new information and incorporates it into existing cognitive schemata, constructing new knowledge and understandings. The key mechanism in learning here is the individual's internal mental structures and processes, and the job of the teacher is to present information in ways which appeal to and extend these.

One of the most influential theorists (particularly in Britain) to apply a cognitive stance to pedagogy was David Ausubel (1969; 1963), who employed an approach variously called expository teaching, reception learning and assimilation theory. Like Piaget and Vygotsky before him, Ausubel was interested in the process by which new ideas are formed and incorporated into existing schemata. His starting point is the statement that 'the most important single factor influencing learning is what the learner already knows' (Ausubel, 1968). It is worth dwelling on this seemingly simple statement, as it obscures something more radical and counter-intuitive. Our instinct, as educationalists, is often to focus on the things we want learners to understand, the new information we aim to introduce. Ausubel, however, cautions against this impulse. Instead, he advocates that our focus be on existing understandings and schemata into which these new ideas will be incorporated – or to use his terminology, subsumed. The result of this process, he maintains, is a richer, more genuine and more meaningful learning. Without it, the best that can occur is surface rote learning (performance, without any deep understanding); at worst, the new understanding – without anything to be anchored in – will be quickly forgotten.

Ausubel's initial claim has strong pedagogic implications, suggesting that learning experiences should begin by activating learners' existing understandings before developing and extending them. This, he argues, should be formally enshrined in an **advanced organizer** – a statement, introduced at the beginning of the session and displayed throughout, which clearly signals what new information is to be introduced and how it is to be embedded in previous understanding. Beyond this, however, he gives further pedagogic advice. He maintains that the teacher's job – across a syllabus and within individual sessions – is to carefully structure concepts so as to emphasize their similarities and differences. In this way, the educator gradually organizes understandings so that learners can meaningfully subsume them into their schemata.

In order to guide this process, Ausubel identifies a variety of different forms of subsumption (a parallel might be drawn here with Piaget's adaptation strategies).

- **Derivative subsumption** involves the adding of new cases or examples to an existing concept. For instance, a child may already have a notion of 'tree' – to which the characteristics of 'oak', 'beech', 'fir' and so on are added without the idea of 'tree' being altered particularly.
- **Correlative subsumption** involves adding detail to an existing high-level concept. This is more complex than simply noting the shape and colour of oak or beech leaves (this would be derivative subsumption); instead, it involves modifying the higher-concept of 'tree' to include the potential of leaves of different shapes and sizes.
- **Superordinate subsumption** introduces a new higher-level concept within which other existing categories are integrated. For instance, the child might be introduced to the concept of an 'evergreen tree', within which he or she then subsumes and organizes existing lower-level examples of 'tree' (pine, fir, etc.).
- **Combinational subsumption** involves cross-pollinating of ideas from one higher-level category to another. Having established in chemistry, for instance, that oils freeze at lower temperatures than water, the child might start to form a better understanding of how pine oils enable the tree to resist frosts and freezes.

Here, then, Ausubel is noting that the relationship between a new and existing concept is not straightforward. New concepts can be subordinate to existing ones (as in derivative and correlative subsumption), ordinate to them (as in combinational subsumption) or existing above them (superordinate subsumption). It is crucial that teachers are aware of these relationships and that they organize their lessons and teaching around them.

For Ausubel, then, the role of the educator is to present understandings in a way that appeals to the cognitive processes underpinning learning – an imperative also emphasized elsewhere by Robert Gagné (1977). Here, though, a more prescriptive structure is provided, one stipulating that any session of instruction should be based around nine 'events'.

1. No learning can occur if the learner is not interested. Therefore, the first stage is to **gain attention** of the students and pique their curiosity. Thus, the educator should begin the session with some form of 'hook' – for instance, an interesting fact or intriguing question or stimulus for the student to consider.
2. Once the learner is interested and curious, the teacher can **introduce the learning objectives** of the session. These, according to Gagné, should be concrete and bounded – specifically defining what the learner will do, and be able to do, by the end of the session.
3. Once students know the intentions of the session, the educator should **activate prior understanding**. In a stance similar to Ausubel's, Gagné argues that embedding new concepts in existing schemata aids their meaningful storage and, hence, recall. In practice, this stage might simply involve questioning learners about prior experiences and understandings.
4. It is only at this point that the learner will be cognitively prepared – and the educator can **present new material**. Gagné argues that the same information should be presented in different ways – for instance, verbally or in video or diagram – to appeal to different learning styles.
5. Gagné suggests that, alongside new concepts and ideas, learners also be given **guidance** as to how best to understand and remember the new ideas. This might, for instance, be given in the form of illustrations or analogies – comparisons –or memory tricks, such as a mnemonic.
6. While the teacher-led understanding produced so far can be effective, Gagné argues that it will be limited until the learner has had an opportunity to personalize and apply ideas. Thus, the next stage should be to **elicit performance**, allowing learners to deploy their understandings and, in doing so, encode and refine them in a way which will encourage retention.
7. As individuals work to apply their ideas, the educator should monitor and analyse their performance, **providing feedback** which will encourage a more

effective and accurate understanding. In other words, formative assessment should be provided.

8. Once the unit of learning has been completed, a form of **summative assessment** should be provided in which performance will be unaided by feedback or support.

9. At the end of the instructional sequence, activities should be given to **enhance retention and transfer**. These might, for instance, involve applying the ideas to unfamiliar and real-life contexts.

There are clear parallels between the pedagogical advice given by Ausubel and Gagné. Both emphasize the role of the teacher in carefully structuring sessions and organizing knowledge to enhance and appeal to cognitive processes. Their loci differ slightly, with Ausubel focusing on the structure and relationships of concepts and Gagné emphasizing the manipulation of the learners' cognitive state. Both tend, however, to be teacher-centred in their leanings, in that the educator is the point of focus – though, of course, both see the learner as an active agent (unlike behavioural approaches).

Other cognitive pedagogies are more fundamentally student-centred; the work of the American psychologist Jerome Bruner (1990; 1986; 1966; 1960) is particularly pertinent in this respect. In line with the core beliefs of cognitive psychology, Bruner sees the learner as an active agent; he emphasizes the importance of existing schemata in guiding learning. However, where Ausubel and Gagné emphasize the importance of the teacher in micromanaging student perception and structuring knowledge in a meaningful way, Bruner argues that students should be presented with learning experiences which encourage them to discern the structure of subject content for themselves. In doing so, they should discover the links and relationships between different facts, concepts and theories (rather than have the teacher simply tell them). By carefully presenting challenges in this way, Bruner argues, children will be encouraged to go beyond the understandings they already have, extrapolating and hypothesizing as they do so. It is this process, he maintains, that is key to learning.

Based on this core principle, Bruner developed the concept of **discovery learning**, arguing that students should 'not be presented with subject matter in its final form, but required to organize it themselves . . .

[requiring them] to discover for themselves relationships that exist among items of information' (Bruner, 1961). The result is an extremely active form of learning, in which the students are always engaged in tasks such as finding patterns or solving puzzles and in which they constantly need to exercise their existing schemata, reorganizing and amending concepts to address the challenges of the tasks.

Bruner's theory is probably best illustrated with an example. The instinctive response of a teacher to the task of helping a child understand the concepts of odd and even numbers, for instance, would be to explain the difference to them. Bruner, however, would argue that an understanding of the concept would be much more genuine if the child discovered the difference for himself. This may be realized, for instance, by playing a game in which the child must share a number of beads between himself and a friend.

On the surface, Bruner's emphasis on learners discovering subject content for themselves seemingly absolves the teacher of a great deal of work. In practice, however, his model requires the teacher to be actively involved in lessons, creating a scaffolded environment which will facilitate learning on the part of the student. On one hand, this involves the selection and design of appropriate stimulus materials and activities which the student can understand and complete. However, Bruner is also an advocate of the teacher's active involvement in the 'business' of the classroom, circulating to work with individual students to perform six core functions (Wood et al., 1976):

- **Recruitment**: ensuring that each student is interested in the task and understands what is required of him or her.
- **Reducing degrees of freedom**: helping the student make sense of the material by eliminating irrelevant directions and thus reducing the trial-and-error aspect of learning.
- **Direction maintenance**: ensuring that the learner is on-task and interest is maintained, often by breaking the ultimate aim of the task into 'sub-aims' which are more readily understood and achieved.
- **Marking critical features**: highlighting relevant concepts or processes and pointing out errors.
- **Frustration control**: stopping students from giving up on the task.
- **Demonstration**: providing models for imitation or possible (partial) solutions.

In context, Bruner's model might be better described as *guided* discovery learning, as the teacher is vital in ensuring that acquisition of new concepts and processes is successful. Within the framework, it is possible to discern both a Piagetian and a Vygotskian legacy. Underpinning discovery learning, for instance, is the need to push children to go beyond what they already know by presenting environments which encourage hypothesizing, extrapolation and problem solving – akin to Piaget's notion of disequilibrium. At the same time, however, Bruner places a Vygotsky-like emphasis on interaction and scaffolding from the teacher.

Bruner also argues that scaffolding needs to occur in a wider sense, that education should follow a **spiral curriculum**. The underlying principle here is that the learner should revisit particular concepts and ideas over and over again during the educative experience, each time building on understanding and requiring more sophisticated cognitive strategies (and thus increasing the sophistication of understanding). He argues that as children age, they are capable of increasingly complex **modes of representation** – basically, ways of thinking – and the spiral curriculum should be sensitive to this development.

- Initially, children learn better using an **enactive** mode of representation (i.e., they learn better through doing things, such as physical and manual tasks). The concept of addition, for instance, might first be taught by asking the child to combine piles of beads and count the results.
- As they grow older – and more familiar with subject content – pupils become more confident in using an **iconic** mode of representation – they are able to perform tasks by imagining concrete pictures in their heads. To continue the example above, as the child becomes more confident with addition, he should be able to imagine the beads in order to complete additions without physically needing to manipulate the piles.
- Finally, students become capable of more abstract, **symbolic** modes of representation, without the need for either physical manipulation or mental imagery. Consequently, at this point the student should have little problem with completing a series of written calculations involving numbers which are higher than can possibly be manipulated by imagining beads.

For Bruner, then, it is the responsibility of educators – be they teachers or curriculum designers – to consider learning experiences in the short, medium and long terms alike. They should structure these experiences around the principle of revisiting and complicating particular understandings multiple times, while remaining mindful of progression not only in content but also in the learner's modes of representation.

Stop, Think, Do

Drawing on one of the cognitive frameworks introduced so far, use its principle to devise a plan for a lesson. Use an alternative framework to devise a plan that has the same focus but follows different principles. Use these two lesson plans to critically compare your chosen models.

Influence, legacies and controversies

As with the behavioural stance, the constructivist approach to learning has had – and continues to have – a significant influence on educational policy and practice. However, unlike the behavioural approach – which lends itself to procedural shaping of behaviour and thus classroom management – the cognitive stance begins to give insight into the underlying processes by which understandings are formed and developed. Hence, advocates for the approach argue that a careful application of its principles gives a much more powerful understanding of the processes by which learning occurs *inside* the minds of learners – and thus of the potential to actively manage this process.

At its most basic, the central message of the constructivist approach is that learning is an active process of 'meaning making'. The implication here is that learners must be challenged and engaged and that this process must occur in the context of new information which is meaningful and related to existing understandings if new understandings are to be formed. Such a stance is in stark contrast to the kinds of repetitive, meaningless, rote learning promoted by behavioural approaches and common in the early phases of state education. From the late 1950s, as unease with rote learning and the stranglehold of behaviourism over education grew, practice was increasingly oriented to a more constructivist stance. This came to a head in the 1960s with a report from the Central Advisory Council for Education (Plowden, 1967), which emphasized the efficacy of constructivist approaches. This heavily influential paper signalled the high-point of a so-called progressive era in education, one championing constructivist principles are their most extreme. Thus, there was an emphasis on student-initiated and discovery learning (influenced by the likes of Bruner) and on mixed ability and peer teaching (drawing on the work of Vygotsky).

Many interpret that era as a golden age of innovative pedagogy; indeed, many of the practices with which teachers experimented in that phase of history have been recurrent since then. It is, though, possible to overly romanticize the pedagogy's impact and extent, and doing so ignores the significant critique that constructivist approaches amassed through the late 1970s and early 1980s. At the more conservative end of this critique was a concern that in the push for open-ended and student-initiated learning, fundamentals were not being taught in schools. A lack of 'direct teaching' of such aspects of the curriculum as literacy and the times tables was, according to critics, leaving a generation of school children ill equipped for their future place in the economy. Further, critiques attacked the mixed-ability mantra of progressive education, declaring that such an approach failed to meet the needs of the less able and failed to challenge the more talented learners.

A separate wave of criticism held that the practices derived from a commitment to constructivism rarely matched the ideals and principles that inspired them. Teachers lacked the skill to properly manage mixed-ability groups or meet the needs of every learner in a child-initiated and discovery-based context. Arguably, this was compounded by large class sizes, which meant that the workload associated with the approach was unworkable. The result was a watered-down and ineffective middle-ground, an incoherent mixture of constructivist ideals and traditionalist practices.

Criticism of the constructivist, progressive movement came to a head in the late 1960s and early 1970s with a series of publications by leading figures detailing the 'excesses' of progressive education. Collectively known as the 'black papers' (Cox and Dyson, 1971), these publications lamented falling standards and behaviour in school (and the malign influence of 'left-wing' teachers) and called for a return to more traditional approaches to education. Their influence continued through the 1980s and into the 1990s, alongside increasingly centralized control over curriculum and pedagogy.

This movement saw a reining in of constructivist principles in education – but not their eradication. A more toned-down manifestation remained throughout, one typically drawing on a more Ausubelian approach. Hence, an emphasis on the meaningfulness of learning was never lost and remains present today. The most notable example of this was the rise of the 'learning objective' (and corresponding 'objective board') – a principle derived directly from Ausubel's notion of advanced organizers. A similar strand runs through the attempts by government agencies to arrange concepts progressively and logically in the literacy and numeracy strategies (though this, in itself, is a point open to critique). More recently, there has been closer attention paid to the micro details of how children construct 'rules' of subjects (e.g. teachers are expected to attend to the formation of 'misconceptions' in maths), an approach clearly influenced by schema theory.

In the period since 2000, there have been signs of another wave of progressive forms of constructivism. The emphasis on meaningful learning, for instance, has raised the possibility of teaching children through content and activities in which they are already interested; for instance, by drawing on characters and concepts from popular culture (cf. Marsh and Millard, 2000). Similarly, new approaches to the Early Years and Foundation stage of education have placed more emphasis on child-initiated learning and on the importance of discovery than on taught content for the earliest years of educational experience.

Summary and conclusions

The behavioural and cognitive approaches represent the most established dimensions of learning theory; in this respect, they have been deeply influential. Many other fundamental debates on education can be mapped onto the competing principles of each – the teacher versus student-centred approach, for instance, or the traditional versus progressive approach. Each approach has attracted controversy, though each maintains an influence in education which shapes practice and policy in fundamental ways. This is not, however, to maintain that either of these perspectives is 'right' nor that they are mutually exclusive. Indeed, a pragmatic educational practice probably borrows liberally from each. Equally, while these approaches define 'conventions' in learning theory, they are not the only source of understanding learning, whether as an outcome or a process.

In the next chapter we turn our attention to some of the new directions which have emerged in learning theory over the past twenty years.

Key questions

- What conventions have been established in understanding the process and experience of learning?
- To what extent should learning be understood as an external process of 'conditioning'?
- How might notions of schemata and internal cognition be useful in understanding learning?
- What are the key overlaps and distinctions in these theoretical frameworks, and how do their contrasts expose underlying tensions in the ways that we understand learning?
- How have conventions in learning theory left legacies in educational policy and practice?
- What controversies have surrounded the legacies left by key learning theories?

Further reading

Ausubel, D. (1963). *The Psychology of Meaningful Verbal Learning*. New York: Grune and Stratton.

Bandura, A. (1977). *Social Learning Theory*. Englewood Cliffs, NJ: Prentice Hall.

Bruner, J. (1966). *Toward a Theory of Instruction*. Cambridge, MA: Harvard University Press.

Gagné, R. (1977). *Conditions of Learning*. Andover, MA: Thomson Learning.

Greene, D., B. Sternberg and M. Lepper (1976). 'Overjustification in a token economy'. *Journal of Personality and Social Psychology*, 34, 1219–34.

Harris, B. (1979). 'Whatever happened to Little Albert?'. *American Psychologist*, 34, 151–60.

Marsh, J., and E. Millard (2000). *Literacy and Popular Culture: Using Children's Culture in the Classroom*. London, Sage.

Piaget, J. (1985). *The Equilibration of Cognitive Structures: The Central Problem of Intellectual Development*. Chicago: University of Chicago Press.

Skinner, B. (1988). *About Behaviourism*. New York: Random House.

Vygotsky, L. (1987). *Thought and Language*. Cambridge, MA: MIT Press.

2 Learning Theories: New Directions

The ideas explored in the previous chapter go some way towards forming the foundations and conventions of learning theory. They are precepts in understanding the processes and experiences of learning which, as explored, have left an important legacy, shaping various facets of educational institutions and practices – and they continue to do so in overwhelming ways. This said, no field is ever static, and thus theories of learning have continued to evolve and develop. This chapter examines a selection of the theoretical 'turns' which are giving direction and trajectory to the future of learning theory. In some respects, these developments have been paradigmatic – building on existing conventions in constructivism and behaviourism. Elsewhere, however, the shifts have been more radical; proposing not just refinements to understandings but also entirely new foundations to the process and experience.

Cognitive processes

One set of developments in learning theory relates to a refinement of existing understandings and models; the tradition of constructivism has seen particular growth in this respect. As explored in the previous chapter, foundational theorists such as Vygotsky and Piaget have outlined very general principles of schema formation and development, while others such as Ausubel and Bruner have taken these into classroom pedagogy. More contemporary theorists have attempted to dig deeper into these processes and the dynamics by which information interacts with existing schemata in order to generate new understandings. This chapter examines a selection of these contributions.

Elaboration theory

One attempt to refine and extend the constructivist stance on learning and to apply it to the classroom context was provided by Charles Reigeluth (1987; 1992), whose approach follows the legacy established by Ausubel (as it focuses very much on the way teachers structure knowledge in their instructional designs). Thus, Reigeluth places emphasis on the sequencing of content as the primary mechanism governing the efficacy of learning, arguing that any instruction should begin with 'epitomes', the key notions of the subject represented in simple ways (note that this is different from 'summarizing' them). In some cases, these epitomes might be procedures – for instance, 'baking a cake' always has a basic structure of action. Equally, though, they can be conceptual; in teaching the basic principles of the psychology of learning, for instance, one could start with the fundamental features which distinguish behavioural and constructivist approaches.

Having established a sound understanding of the epitomes of the learning – and Reigeluth places heavy emphasis on forming a confident and meaningful understanding of them – it is then possible to 'drill down' within key ideas and add detail, variation, sub-perspective and so on. Thus, the epitome sets the basis for a new layer of learning which, itself, has a series of epitomes which can then form the basis for additional layers. Throughout this process, it is necessary to draw together these hierarchical concepts, so that learners maintain a sense of their overall interrelatedness. Reigeluth advocates a number of strategies to accomplish this goal, including two parallel processes:

- Summary: the presentation of ideas so far. Summary can be 'internal', that is, focused on a particular lesson, or 'within set' – which draws on concepts from the whole sequence of lessons.

- Synthesis: encouraging students to combine and recombine ideas themselves with a view to producing new understandings which, in turn, expose interrelationships within the content.

Throughout, Reigeluth notes that learners should be in active control of their learning in terms of pace and form of engagement with the sequence. Further, they should be developing particular transferable 'cognitive-strategies' through which to transform and make sense of learning; these might be embedded into the instruction (e.g. the presentation of analogies) or *detached*, with the learners themselves required to exercise a previously learned skill ('formulate your own analogy', for instance).

Reigeluth's model provides a useful framework through which teachers can design programmes of instruction in systematic ways, and its key strength is, perhaps, that it offers guidance which is more contained and easily followed than that of Ausubel. That it is focused on *instructional* design is, however, also its greatest drawback; while the approach is useful in teaching causal understandings and absolute facts, it tends towards convergent understandings. Thus, it precludes the possibility of encouraging divergent thinking – beyond that which is predefined in the epitomes around which learning has been structured.

Stop, Think, Do

Consider the way in which a particular subject area of your choosing might be reduced to epitomes. Having identified these facets, how would you proceed to design a programme of instruction?

Metacognition

In our explorations of constructivism so far, the cognitive strategies through which individuals appropriate and incorporate new understandings have been treated as fundamentally private and internal structures. As a result, the pedagogies that they inspire have, in effect, placed the teacher in a privileged position, with an expert understanding of these hidden processes and an ability to manipulate them in order to promote learning. A growing school of theorists and practitioner is, however, beginning to challenge this 'top-down' arrangement of expertise. They note that giving learners insight into their own learning processes will let them acquire understandings in a more autonomous and effective way.

The notion of metacognition – first introduced by John Flavell (1979; 1987) – explores the way in which individuals think about and self-regulate their own processes of thinking and learning. Within this basic definition, it is possible to draw two distinct strands of metacognition (after Brown, Bransford, Ferrara and Campione, 1983). On the one hand, it involves monitoring the specific process of learning as a contained event (that is, for instance, as it occurs within lessons). At the most simple, this involves building up a repertoire of understanding of cognitive systems and a series of associated strategies through which to better engage with these underlying processes. Learners might be taught, for instance, about the basics of schema theory, then coached in the effective use of mind maps in order to organize and represent schemata, or about the ways in which memory works. They might also be taught strategies through which to independently engage with resources, such as written texts, in ways which ensure that they are cognitively active. An example of this form of strategy is SQ3R (Robin, 1970), in which learners are given a system through which to read that consists of five steps[1]:

- Survey: The reader spends a couple of minutes looking over the text and getting a sense of its structure and key features (headings, pictures, etc.).
- Question: A series of key questions is then formulated in response to this overview, to which the reader is actively attempting to answer.
- Read: At this point, learners works their way through the chapter – at all times, keeping the key questions in mind.
- Recite/Write: Once reading is completed, the learners write down key summary points (in their own words) and answers to their original questions.

---

[1] Interestingly, SQ3R was originally proposed in the 1930s – though it emerged as a pedagogic strategy that worked rather than a theory-based construct. The emerging interest in metacognition has, however, led to a revival in these forms of study skill-type approaches.

- Review: Having completed this phase, the readers cover their notes and test the extent to which they have remembered key ideas – returning to notes and the original text as necessary.

The key idea here – and in metacognitive strategies more generally – is to ensure that learners themselves regulate an active engagement with their learning and, in doing so, manage the formation of well-structured schemata. In addition to cognitive awareness, these strategies can be coupled with other modes of self-regulation, which might minimize variables that interfere with learning – for instance, by teaching learners to monitor and manage levels of negative emotions, such as frustration.

The second strand of metacognition relates to a more general monitoring and self-regulation of knowledge, reasoning and understanding – outside specific bounded-learning events. In this respect, metacognition relates to self-awareness about what one knows and doesn't know – and those ideas that are clear and those that require further elaboration. It also involves the ability to act in response to these understandings, to independently seek out and clarify understandings and to address areas of weakness and extended and developing areas of strength. Facilitating this set of skills makes very particular pedagogical demands – and it might be argued that even where classrooms are 'student-centred', the extent of this is rarely sufficient to develop metacognition fully. Assessment and differentiation of content, for instance, tend to remain fundamentally the responsibility of teachers, and thus learners are 'deskilled' and separated from the key processes underpinning this dimension of metacognition. Reflective learning therefore implicates a more fundamentally radical student-centred shift, with self-assessment as a central process and an open-ended learning environment in which learners are able to actively seek out understandings they deem necessary.

As a theoretical principle, the idea of metacognition adds an important dimension to our understanding of learning. Elsewhere, constructivist approaches have described learning as an active process, but the learners themselves are left without any control over the underlying systems by which this occurs. Metacognition adds precisely this dimension to the theoretical framework and, in doing so, distances the approach from an empty 'information processing' model which sees the learner robotically encountering information in a pre-programmed way. The approach also has useful pedagogical implications which have the potential to enrich and improve learning. It actively attempts to empower learners to be autonomous and self-directed, and thus, it may produce a form of learning which is more sustainable beyond direct educational experience. Compared with the kind of instructional approaches advocated by Reigeluth and Ausubel, the pedagogies inspired by metacognition are more open ended and divergent and emphasize problem solving, rather than the convergence on particular pre-determined answers. The notion of metacognition has consequently gained influence in mainstream pedagogy in recent years, both at the level of individual teaching practice and in official policy. The introduction of *The Assessment for Learning Strategy* (DCSF, 2008), for instance, was intended to increase the use of formative assessment – that which feeds back into learning – rather than summative assessment – which merely summarizes achievements – and place a degree of emphasis on peer and self-assessment.

The concept and consequent pedagogies, however, are not perfect, and they possess important flaws. Most notably, facilitating the kinds of self-directed learning suggested by advocates of metacognition is far from simple. It requires the development in learners of critical and reflective skills; they must be taught how to reflect and self-assess skilfully and honestly before they can seek out their own understandings. Failure to instil these abilities can result in a surface approximation of the processes put forward by the approach; pupils might, for instance, 'perform' self-assessment in ways distorted by social pressures (such as an unwillingness to reveal uncertainty). Further, the approach over-emphasizes the extent to which learning is governed by conscious metacognition. It may well be that the strategies and procedures it advocates are effective in improving learning within the context of the classroom – as a very particular context – but when transposed to more organic everyday contexts, habit and convention (rather than explicit metareasoning) may be more overwhelming pressures.

> ### Stop, Think, Do
>
> Use the principles of SQ3R, introduced above, as a structure through which to read the remainder of this chapter.

The social turn

Perhaps one of the most interesting developments in the emphasis of learning theory over the past 25 years has been an emergent focus on social aspects – a recognition that the fundamentally 'individualist' model of learning, which has dominated learning theory for a century, is flawed in that it fails to fully attend to the nature of interaction between people as a fundamental process. Two emergent perspectives might be seen to be emblematic of the directions that can be taken by these emerging schools.

Dialogic teaching

While conventional models of learning have been fundamentally individualist, they have made overtones to 'the social'. Such reference can be found, for instance, in the imitation of others in Bandura's theory or the need for interaction in that of Vygotsky. It is from the legacy of the latter of these perspectives that our first social stance on learning develops – though, as we explore later, they also make an important theoretical break from it. A growing school of theorists, notably Robin Alexander and Neil Mercer, begin their analysis by emphasizing the medium through which individuals interact with one another. They argue that a better understanding of learning can be gleaned only through a better understanding of how individuals talk and use language as a tool to mediate and facilitate thought.

Where Vygotsky talked in general terms about the importance of language to learning, however, these approaches attempt a degree of greater sensitivity, recognizing that not all interaction is equal in its qualities or effects. As such, they set out to explore the nature of different forms of 'talk' on learning – drawing heavily on empirical observations of how individuals communicate with one another inside of classrooms.

Alexander (2001), for instance, conducted a cross-cultural examination of classroom talk – comparing France, India, Russia, the United States and England. On the basis of this work, he identifies five distinct categories of language use in the official 'business' of school:

- rote – the repetition of facts and ideas in order to learn them through drill;
- recitation – the questioning of pupils in order to elicit recall or to encourage pupils to discover a set answer in order to reinforce or extend knowledge;
- instruction/exposition – direct explanation of information or procedures;
- discussion – the sharing of information with a view to solving problems;
- dialogue – the use of structured and cumulative questioning and discussion in order to reach a common understanding.

An important point to note here is that Alexander and his contemporaries identify something more than 'surface activity' (which might, for instance, tend towards a focus on 'on-task' and 'off-task' discussion). Rather, they explore the deeper pedagogical implications of different forms of talk and the processes by which they structure, mediate and facilitate different forms of learning. A common thread running through this work is that within each of the categories of talk, dialogue-like conversation has the potential to have the most profound impact on a learner's thinking – though equally common is the observation that space for such activity is often pushed out of the classroom by various institutional and situational constraints, and the other forms of interaction therefore become more prevalent.

The importance of dialogue is based on a definition beyond the everyday sense of 'turn taking' in speech. Rather, it implies an openness of discussion, in order to generate understandings – a dialectic interaction with the meanings on which the discussants draw. Thus, individuals engaged in dialogue are also actively co-constructing knowledge – rather than being given or discovering particular right answers. To draw on the language of Coffin and O'Halloran (2008, 219), the emphasis should be on the *process* of argumentation rather than on the end product of an argument – and on the critical exploration, evaluation and synthesis of meanings that this entails. In engaging with this process, learners should be empowered to take ownership of learning and of the knowledge with which they engage rather than be passive recipients of it.

Within this basic framework of ideas, two distinct remits of focus have emerged: one primarily concerned with the pedagogic implications of teacher–pupil interaction and the other with examining the nature of talk between pupils. Robin Alexander is a particularly prominent voice in the first area of focus. On the basis of carefully executed empirical work, Alexander notes the way in which teacher-talk has been framed and shaped by historical practices – and by particular social constructions of how knowledge is constituted. One interesting facet of these observations is that, in Britain, rhetoric of 'interactive' teaching obscures a reality which is far more static and transmissive, drawing heavily on the historic legacy of rote, recitation and instruction (Alexander, 2008a). In explaining this mismatch of ideal and reality, Alexander notes the ways in which an emphasis on individual participation in classes is undermined by high ratios of students to teachers, which inevitably results in a competitive game of 'guess what the teacher is thinking' and a hunt for a particular 'right' answer (2008a, 106). As such, dialogue is reduced to testing and probing, and there is little or no space for the take-up and development of a student's own contributions (a problem which is, of course, compounded by prescriptive curriculum structures).

It is, however, precisely this process – of taking a learner's contribution as a starting point for extended dialogue – which is, according to Alexander, crucial to deep and effective learning. The traditional pattern of initiation-response-feedback (the IRF model) develops the performance of a set of prescribed ideas but fails to develop any deep thinking about them or the ability to use those ideas in an empowered way. A more dialogical method of teaching, however – with the teacher probing, challenging and extending a set of ideas which are grounded in the learners' contributions – encourages the learners to actively construct knowledge for themselves and to attend to the chains of reason and argument which constitute them. Such an approach therefore encourages a much deeper and more transcendental set of understandings and capacities.

While Alexander's focus has been primarily with the interactions between teachers and pupils, Neil Mercer has emerged as a central thinker with an alternative focus: on the talk that occurs between pupils. Thus, his concern has been with the qualities of interaction which underpin effective collaborative learning – the ways in which talk is connected in order to facilitate 'social modes of thinking'. He identifies three different categories of interaction (Dawes et al., 2000):

- disputational talk – characterized by a competiveness between participants; the attempt to validate individual points of view, rather than exchange understandings;
- cumulative talk – in which participants add to each others contributions in a systematic but uncritical way;
- exploratory talk – based on reason and criticality and on exchange, challenge and counter-challenge of ideas.

True to the precepts identified above, it is the last of these forms of interaction which Mercer sees as most valuable in learning. Echoing the distinction between argument and argumentation, he emphasizes that the public visibility of the processes of reasoning are the most important pedagogical features of this talk, rather than the actual points being made (which are central to disputational and cumulative talk). This emphasis stresses that learners are thus able to better understand deep meanings and relationships, to consider in more critical ways – drawing on multiple perspectives – and to construct logics and reasoned arguments for themselves.

This form of talk does not, of course, come automatically – and, drawing on Vyogotskian terminology, Mercer emphasizes the role of teachers in scaffolding learners' use of dialogue (Edwards and Mercer, 1987). In this respect, his work suggests that, in many ways, learners adopt the kinds of functions of talk that are deployed by teachers. Thus, he identifies recaps, reformulations, elicitations, repetitions and elaborations as prevalent components of pupils discussions (Mercer, 1995; 2000). Facilitating actively exploratory talk among learners therefore necessitates a break from these closed habits among teachers – and the active striving to create a context which facilitates open questioning and which encourages explicit reasoning over the 'settled-on' answer. This notion of scaffolding is also reflected by Alexander, as is an emphasis on producing an appropriate 'climate' around learning, one which does not ridicule or spend too much time emphasizing failure and thus discourage open and exploratory talk. To this end, Alexander highlights specific components of classroom ethos which are more conducive to dialogic teaching (Alexander, 2008b). He argues that successful classrooms are:

- collective – based on a democratic structure, with teachers and learners addressing tasks together;
- reciprocal – having a genuine exchange of meanings and understandings, based on the principle that ideas shared by others are always considered genuinely;
- supportive – enabling learners to share ideas freely without fear of punishment or of 'the wrong answer'.

The empirical nature of work by theorists such as Alexander and Mercer has enabled them to have significant influence on educational policy and practice – much more so than other endeavours which have been similarly focused (e.g. Freire, 1996; 2001). This is true to the extent that it has spoken to the heart of government policy making and that its principles were included in National Primary and Key Stage 3 strategies. It clearly makes important recommendations, in terms of paying attention to the micro-detail of educational interaction and of the processes by which deep understandings might be formed. As with each of the perspectives in this chapter, however, the legacy of these approaches is yet to be established, and it seems that the realities of their impact might be tempered by material constraints. The pressures of teaching large groups, for instance, which Alexander pinpoints as central to the over-use of didactic teaching methods, are not easily overcome by pedagogical advice alone.

Stop, Think, Do

Working with a partner, attempt a dialogic conversation about the nature of learning. Remember, the key process here is not about arriving at answers or at disagreements, but about finding interesting new ways of thinking about what your partner has said.

Situated learning

There is, then, a sense that this branch of learning theory is communal and socially mediated and that co-construction of understandings is a fundamental educational process. However, the approach retains a fundamentally individualist focus; the nexus of 'understanding' remains clustered in the people doing the interacting. Other approaches have, however, taken this emphasis on the social further, disconnecting learning from specific individuals and instead exploring how groups and communities learn and establish particular bodies of knowledge and understanding. It is to this aspect of theory to which we now turn our attention.

One of the most well-established perspectives in this school was established by Jean Lave and Etienne Wenger (1991; 1998) in the form of 'situated learning'. The starting point of this approach is radical and involves a break from a number of key assumptions that surround conventional learning theory. In the context of this section, the most important is a shift away from an individualist concept of learning, to a socially situated one – a premise that alone is a considerable departure from the ways in which we habitually think about learning. Beyond this, however, Lave and Wenger encourage their readers to imagine learning as something that is not bounded by the institution and processes of 'school'. Thus, they envisage learning as something organic and ongoing and embedded in various **communities of practice** with which individuals engage throughout their lives. A community of practice can refer to any group that a learner participates in – though they are more than just networks or associations. Rather, they are communities of individuals with a commitment to a particular domain of interest and, in turn, to a set of practices which evolve around that domain – ways of understanding and making sense of experiences, of addressing common problems and so on.

Defined in this way, communities of practice range greatly and include traditional classroom communities, professionals (such as teachers or doctors) and even leisure-pursuit communities (e.g. around sports and even around the playing of computer games). The work of Lave and Wenger thus involves the study of a whole range of 'apprenticeships' – from midwives to butchers and members of alcoholics anonymous. These communities range in their fluidity and formality, and some are seen by society as more legitimate and worthwhile than others. For Lave and Wenger, however, these variables are ultimately immaterial; regardless of their status and recognition and of their level of stability, these communities are sites of learning for those involved in them – and thus, areas in which interesting processes occur.

For Lave and Wenger, notions of identity and participation are inseparable from that of learning – and their analysis therefore begins not with a consideration of internal cognitive processes nor of individualized external behaviours but with the importance of social interactions. Knowledge, in this respect, is not something acquired; rather it is something generated by the community in order to facilitate particular practices. Within that community, certain arrays of practice and understanding may accumulate and attain a state of dogma. Thus, particular sets of languages, symbols, concepts and routines become conventions, both in behaviours and in forming the 'glue' that binds together individuals within that particular community. In nascent communities, these conventions must be actively achieved, but in most cases they are more established, and new members therefore join that community by learning to engage with and within them. Lave and Wenger coin the phrase 'legitimate peripheral participation' to describe this process; it implies an engagement which is partial, but still substantial, before it progresses to full participation. A key point here is that this is not just a case of learning the rules; the very act of participation is crucial, as it involves the development of relationships and affiliations which sustain the group. Further, participation is not just a process of learning to 'talk like' the members of the community but also of being able to 'talk to' them. Thus, it is not simply a case of appropriating and deploying acceptable discourse but also of innovating and improvising. Doing so, however, requires a degree of competence, being able to talk in ways which are 'reasonable' within the languages and parameters of the community.

The key advantage to this approach to learning is that it encompasses a much broader array of human experiences – giving insight into the processes that govern informal learning outside of schools. Notably, it provides a useful set of tools through which to explore the ways in which professional learning takes place. Trainee teachers, for instance, could be seen as engaging in 'legitimate periphery participation', exploring the concepts and routines of their profession in a contained way. Ultimately, they reach a point of full participation, in which they are competent enough to operate within the community with autonomy and innovation (competence is crucial in this, or else the resultant practice will not be meaningful to the community at large).

Lave and Wenger's model also provides an interesting framework through which to analyse more formal contexts of education. It is interesting to consider, for instance, the extent to which 'the school' forms a community of practice and to which the learners within it are learning to play the game of learning as it is defined by that community. When viewed through this lens, the writing of essays, the undertaking of exams and participation in classroom activity become rituals – and learners are more accepted by the community if they can adequately perform these rituals. Those who reach levels of full participation in the community are able to continue to exist within it (moving on to university and beyond) while others move sideways into alternative communities of practice (such as those in workplaces). Such an analysis is reminiscent of the critical treatment of schooling as an institution given earlier by Ivan Illich (1973).

The influence of the approach on mainstream education is, however, limited. In part, this is because its rupture from an individualist model of learning is too radical to be easily accommodated by the conventions of schooling. There are, however, also theoretical ambiguities and problems with the approach. Most notably, it struggles to accommodate value in any transcendental knowledge which is not directly related to 'practice' and does not arise from a specific community. Further, it tends towards an overly idealized conceptualization of the community as a benign entity. As such, little space is given to conceive of groups as actively unsupportive or hierarchical, and the nature and influence of power within, and surrounding, groups is left uninterrogated. 'In their eagerness to debunk testing, formal education and formal accreditation, they do not analyse how their omission affects power relations, access, public knowledge and public accountability' (Tennant, 1997, 97).

Regardless of these criticisms, however, the notions of Lave and Wenger – and of the broader social turn in learning theory – represent an important challenge to the assumptions made about how understanding and knowledge are constituted and acquired. Arguably, this challenge troubles individualist assumptions of learning, which arise as much from a set of institutional assumptions about how they *should* occur as they do from any intrinsic truth about how they *do* occur, and in this respect their arguments are crucial to the theoretical debate surrounding them.

Distributed cognition

The social turn in learning theory is therefore significant in that it situates learning in processes external to any given individual and instead positions it as an interactional process between individuals. Elsewhere, this process of abstracting thinking and learning to a level above that of distinct individuals has been taken further. Thus, in Edwin Hutchins's theory of distributed cognition (1995), learning and thinking are not just constructs of interactions between people but also between those individuals and the objects and artefacts in their environment.

At the basis of this theory is an attempt to understand how 'intelligent action' comes to occur in real-life settings; for Hutchins, problem solving in work-based settings was a prime focus. In exploring this remit, he draws on an anthropological rather than a psychological lens – emphasizing artefacts of cultures over internal constructs of mind. As a result, he sees the traditional view of thought, as something contained within the individual, as flawed – but equally, that thinking is more than just a product of interactions between individuals. Rather, he argues, cognition as it happens in the real world is something that draws on an array of physical artefacts and tools, both to represent ideas and to calculate and manipulate them (what he calls transduction). In his seminal work, Hutchins illustrates this point in reference to the ways that intelligent cognition is achieved in the navigation of ships and aircraft. In both of these cases, teams of individuals work together, mediated by various high and low technologies.

These proposals can speak directly to formal educational practices, which generally see technology as an adjunct to cognition or even as an obstacle to it (consider, for instance, the generally negative ways in which calculators are perceived). Distributed cognition would argue, however, that interaction with these artefacts – and with other people around them – is an intrinsic and inseparable part of the cognition itself. Such a process is actually quite familiar when placed in the context of less-contentious technology. In collaboratively working through a maths question, for instance, learners will often write their calculations on a piece of paper, and in this way, we can see the principles of distributed cognition. On one hand, writing provides a technology to permit communication of ideas between two individuals; at the same time, it provides a mechanism to facilitate calculation and thus cognition. According to Gavriel Salomon (1993), the first of these uses of technology could be seen as shared cognition, while the second is an example of offloading (offsetting some of the labour of thinking to a technology). Viewed in this way, the use of calculators in maths or the use of the internet to support the writing of an essay seem entirely reasonable, though these practices are often stigmatized in formal education. Distributed cognition would hold that such a stigmatization is blind to the realities of how thinking actually occurs in settings beyond schools, colleges and universities and thus calls for pedagogies which support learners in the effective use of cultural tools and artefacts.

There is, of course, an ambiguity at the heart of distributed cognition; namely, over the extent to which thinking, in the theory's model, is something genuinely distributed or whether what it identifies is the cumulative sum of an array of individual thought. Thus, in the example of children working together above (and in Hutchins's original examples), the claim is that the thinking that occurs is only possible at the level of interaction. Equally, though, this interaction could simply facilitate the communication of individually bounded thoughts. Regardless, however, the approach offers an interesting challenge to constructs of thought and learning and an insightful refrain from the impulse to demonize the internet and other technologies used in schools.

Connectivism

The discussion so far in this chapter has challenged some fundamental assumptions; that, for instance, learning has its locus as a process internal to specific individuals (or, in the case of the previous discussion, even that it necessarily inheres in people). A similarly iconoclastic stance is proposed by George Siemens (2005), beginning with the observation that while conventional theories debate the mechanisms through which learning occurs, they all fundamentally agree that those mechanisms (whatever they might be) are universal and unchanging. This reasoning, he suggests, is flawed, because it ignores the way that the relevance and application of knowledge – and, by extension the ways in which individuals must engage with it – shift according to economic, political and technological pressures which are socially and historically specific.

To illustrate, the models of instruction proposed by Ausubel and Reigeluth (and, to a lesser extent, by Bruner's spiral curriculum) imply that knowledge is hierarchical and cumulative – with learners therefore accumulating it by gradually refining and extending tree-like schemata before taking this knowledge forward to sustain their futures outside of education. Thus, learning theories are built on a notably modernist outlook, one mediated by a set of technologies (such as print) which are inherently fixed, linear and hierarchical. However, according to Siemens, economic shifts challenge this view of knowledge; the notion of a 'career for life' is a thing of the past, and thus the view that understandings accumulated in school will sustain a learner throughout life therefore seems outdated. In Siemens's view, the 'half life' of knowledge has been reduced, and individuals must learn and relearn on an ongoing basis. This has, of course, been facilitated by parallel technological changes; the rise of the internet has made society information rich, availing a vast array of knowledge to the individual.

Siemens therefore re-imagines learning not as an accumulation of understanding in readiness for later life but as an ongoing process by which connections are forged between ideas, contexts and experiences. These connections are not necessarily hierarchical, and neither do they respect boundaries between subjects. Rather, they are spontaneous, organic and evolving – erupting in the subjective experience of the learner and against a backdrop of necessity. In a similar stance, Deleuze and Guattari (1980) posit that understandings should be imagined as rhizomes (like a root of ginger) shooting off in unpredictable ways, rather than being forced to conform to a modernist assumption of order. Interestingly, here the notion of networks, nodes and connections – facets of new technology which are seen to transform the nature of knowledge – become mirrored in the construct of learning, which becomes the capacity to forge and maintain these connections.

Given this context, the ability to seek out, appraise and incorporate understandings becomes increasingly important. As Siemens puts it,

> Our ability to learn what we need for tomorrow is more important than what we know today. A real challenge for any learning theory is to actuate known knowledge at the point of application. When knowledge,

however, is needed, but not known, the ability to plug into sources to meet the requirements becomes a vital skill. (Siemens, 2005)

Such a stance has strong pedagogic implications. It suggests, for instance, that formal education should be less an end in itself and more a form of apprenticeship into an ongoing lifelong process of informal learning. It implicates a shift from an emphasis on subject content or specific capabilities to the nurturing of technological literacy and critical awareness. It also suggests a reversal of the subsidiary nature of informal, learner-generated understandings to 'official content' and an emphasis on these dynamic and reflexive knowledge forms in the classroom.

Siemens's observations on the impact of economic and technological changes are certainly interesting, and his assertion that the very process of learning can be one which is socially and historically specific offers an important new critical refrain to conventional theory. There are, however, a number of ambiguities at the heart of the approach. On one hand, critics have questioned the extent to which the theory describes a model of learning, and the extent to which it subverts this into a discussion of pedagogy or even curriculum (Verhagen, 2006), though the response to this is likely to be that social, economic and technological shifts are themselves eroding this boundary. Elsewhere, other detractors have noted that existing learning theories are more than capable of accommodating the impacts of and engagements with new technologies – undermining the apparent necessity of connectivism (Ally, 2008; Kerr, 2007). Regardless of these criticisms, though, the approach makes interesting proposals and draws important and contemporary issues into debates surrounding learning.

Stop, Think, Do

Consider the ways in which the internet and other information technologies have changed the way you engage in learning. How might educational institutions adapt to orient themselves to realities you have identified in the previous task?

Conclusions

This chapter has explored a range of different contemporary approaches to the exploration of learning. In many of these approaches, the legacy of more conventional and established theory is discernable, but, in equal measure, they have also involved ruptures from these stances and a fundamental re-imagination of what learning is and where it occurs. A common sense emerging from this rupture is that learning is often defined in narrow ways, in terms of the kinds of activities that occur in schools. In equal measure, the assumptions that have structured these institutions (such as the notion that learning should be individual) have shaped how theories of learning have understood the activities that have occurred within them. The shift in focus that has occurred here, then, which recognizes learning as something which can be informal, reflexive and ongoing and which can be situated in the contexts within which individuals operate, as well as their interactions among groups and communities, is therefore crucial, not only in terms of theoretical efficacy but also of the kinds of challenge that these observations can make to pedagogy an policy.

Key questions

- How have contemporary developments in learning theory developed and challenged conventions?
- In what ways have these developments extended schema theory and its implicated pedagogies?
- How has a 'social turn' in learning theory both extended Vygotskian perspectives and offered fundamental challenges to understandings of what constitutes thinking and learning?
- In which ways have a growing number of schools of thought considered the relationships between technology, thinking and learning?

Further reading

Alexander, R. (2008b). Towards Dialogic Teaching: Rethinking Classroom Talk. York: Dialogos.

Edwards, D., and N. Mercer, (1987). *Common Knowledge: The Development of Understanding in the Classroom*. London: Falmer Press.

Hutchins, E. (1995). *Cognition in the Wild*. Cambridge, MA: MIT Press.

Lave, J., and E. Wenger (1998). *Communities of Practice: Learning, Meaning and Identity*. Cambridge, UK: Cambridge University Press.

Mercer, N. (1995). The Guided Construction of Knowledge: Talk Amongst Teachers and Learners. Clevedon: Multilingual Matters.

Salomon, G. (1993). *Distributed Cognitions: Psychological and Educational Considerations*. Cambridge, UK: Cambridge University Press.

3 Intelligence and Capacity

Our focus in this text so far has been on the generic processes and principles which purportedly govern the experience and outcomes of learning. There is, however, a substantial body of theory and argument which maintains that such processes are never experienced in the same way by every individual. Rather, there are distinct characteristics in the personality and psychology of learners which create differences – whether in terms of preferences about what is to be learned, capability at different skills or even learning capacity. It is to these dimensions of learning to which we turn our attention here with an exploration of the nature, history and controversies surrounding the concept of intelligence and the later discursive shift towards 'learning style' as an expression and model of individual differences.

Intelligence

The notion of intelligence is one which seemingly appeals to common sense. After all, everyone suspects that some people are cleverer than others – a notion reinforced in our early experiences with the educational system and seemingly instilled in the examination and qualification system through which we exit it. Beyond this informal nagging belief is a more formalized theoretical construct – the notion of Intelligence as a central facet of human psychology, one describing the individual's capacity to learn. (This contrasts with the content of learning – the knowledge and understanding which we gradually acquire through our education.) The theoretical construct of intelligence describes how much learning content one is capable of acquiring and the level of sophistication with which the individual can transform and deploy this learning. The level to which intelligence has become a normalized concept, however, belies its socially constructed nature; the attribute is a fundamentally theoretical one, and the product of development throughout history. It is fitting here, then, to briefly consider the way in which the construct has developed before critically examining its nature and influence.

Stop, Think, Do

What does the concept of intelligence mean to you? To what extent is education still oriented around this notion? Try to think of some problems and critical perspectives on the idea of intelligence.

The historical context of intelligence

The initial history of intelligence had its origins in the work of a group of pioneers of psychometrics – the attempt to systematically measure human psychology in relation to its basic attributes. The most notable of these, in the context of this chapter, was the British psychologist Francis Galton (1869; 1883), who first proposed the notion that all cognitive abilities were limited by a single fundamental underlying attribute. Influenced by his cousin, Charles Darwin, Galton maintained that this attribute was, in turn, governed by biology and focused initially on head size as the key determinant (here he was influenced by the popular Victorian pseudo-science of phrenology, the measurement of personality according to bumps on the head and its overall shape). He later revised this argument in light of contradictory evidence (and perhaps the diminutive size of his own head!) and shifted the biological determinant of intelligence to the speed at which the nervous system was able to process information. In order to explore this, he devised a series of perceptual tests, among them the speed of one's recognition of colours. Though there is a substantial distance between these ideas and intelligence as we recognize it today, Galton laid down some fundamental building blocks: the idea of a singular, fundamental attribute of cognitive ability; that it is governed by internal processing rather than external measurable features; and that tasks can be devised which measure this attribute in precise ways.

These basic principles were, in turn, taken up by the French psychologists Alfred Binet and (later) Theodore Simon (1916), who had been commissioned by the Parisian authorities to devise a method of ascertaining which children were more suited to a formal education and which needed special provision. After careful pilot studies, Binet concluded that Galton's perceptual tests produced variable and thus unreliable results; he argued instead that more direct measures of cognitive ability were needed. To this end, he devised a series of tasks which anticipated the IQ tests of today: remembering sequences of numbers, filling in missing words, counting and comparing and so on. Fundamental, though, was the notion that these tasks were not just about perception but involved active reasoning – in other words, not just the speed of the nervous system, but also the capabilities of the brain. These tasks were carefully calibrated, creating packages which a 'normal' child of each given age could complete. The formalized result of this process was the publication of the Binet-Simon scale and, with it, the notion that intelligence can be measured with tests of reasoning and expressed against an established average.

These fundamental conceptual and methodological principles remain at the core of intelligence theory and testing, though they have undergone significant revision. Most notable in this early phase was the work of the American Lewis Terman (1916), who produced the Stanford-Binet revision of intelligence testing. This saw significant calibration and improvements to the precision of the test and, significantly, the inclusion of a 'quotient', or score, summarizing the intelligence of the individual in relation to the population average. In designing this aspect of his test, Terman drew on the earlier work of the German William Stern (1914), who had proposed that this intelligence quotient, or IQ, might be measured using a formula: mental age divided by chronological age multiplied by 100. An 'average' individual would thus score 100, and Terman ensured that a majority of the others would score between 80 and 120. Thus, the notion that intelligence was normally distributed (something implied earlier by Galton) was enshrined as a core principle of intelligence testing.

Though revisions continued throughout the twentieth century, the work of Terman saw the establishment of intelligence testing as it is generally expressed today. Some of these revisions were methodological – for instance, the development of separate tests for different age brackets (Wechsler, 1949). Elsewhere, there were further theoretical debates – notably, concerning the ways in which individual 'talents' independent of intelligence might be explained. One of the most famous responses to this problem was given by Charles Spearman (1927) in the form of the 'two-factor' theory of intelligence, which maintains that intellectual capacity is made up of two elements, the person's general intelligence (which Spearman calls g), and his or her individual component abilities. Thus, performance in a particular area will be influenced by specific intelligence in that area, though this in turn will be underpinned by general intelligence.

Other psychologists have disagreed with Spearman's notion that all specific intelligences are predicated on an underlying general intelligence. Thurston (1924), for instance, maintaining that Spearman confused cause and effect, argued that general intelligence is actually based on the combined product of various underlying specific intelligences: verbal comprehension, word fluency, number, space, associative memory and perceptual speed and reasoning. More recently, other theorists – notably Guilford (1967) and Vernon (1950) – have continued these 'component analyses' of general intelligence. Fundamentally, though, what remains is the sense that a general intelligence exists (regardless of its component parts) and that it can be measured using the familiar tests of spatial, logical and mathematical reasoning, the result being a normally distributed set of scores with a mean of 100.

The uses and misuses of IQ

By the early twentieth century, the concept of general intelligence had been normalized, and an array of standardized instruments were available with which to measure the quotient of any given individual. It was consequently inevitable that intelligence would enter the normal discourse of formal education (especially given the relationship between early pioneers of IQ and the state). Such was the pervasiveness of its influence that, when secondary education was first introduced in Britain in 1944, intelligence and IQ testing were at its core. Under the influence of Cyril Burt – the chief government statistics officer and a committed psychometrician – at the end of primary school children were given a test (the 11-plus exam) aimed at diagnosing their academic aptitude and assigning them to a secondary school as appropriate.

This intimate relationship between intelligence as a construct and formal education eventually grew troubled under the weight of criticism of the 11-plus: that it limited life chances at an early age, that it disadvantaged the working classes and that it provided only a narrow and one-dimensional evaluation of pupils. Never again since that point has the exam's influence been so direct and overwhelming, but this is not to say that its influence has evaporated completely. Most obviously and importantly, a belief in intelligence exists in the popular consciousness, and this inevitably influences the behaviour of policymakers and practitioners in subtle ways. There is, too, some use of intelligence testing within the education system, though it tends to be confined to one in a battery of tests used to diagnose special educational needs and as an entry test to private schools and the handful of remaining state-funded grammar schools. In the United States, the systematic and widespread use of aptitude testing is more prevalent, with secondary school students taking the Scholastic Aptitude Test (SAT) as a requirement for university admission. This form of admissions policy has also been tentatively trailed in the United Kingdom; despite the general critique of IQ tests within education, studies reveal that, with careful application, these can more successfully identify able pupils of working-class backgrounds than the more conventional A-level results (McDonald and Newton, 2001).

Beyond direct applications in the formal educational system, the concept of intelligence and the use of IQ testing also had a broader socio-political impact. It is here that some of its darker influences are found. At the core of these controversies is the insistence that intelligence has a genetic foundation – a belief which, in turn, has inspired the eugenics movement, which argues that selective breeding (and sterilization) should be applied to protect the intellectual stock of society. This position has roots in the very foundations of the concept of intelligence – with the work of Galton – though it is important to note that the opposite position – that IQ is as much a product of experience and environmental factors – also has its origins in this early phase. Stephen Jay Gould (1996), for instance, notes that Binet is often lumped together with Galton as an intellectual geneticist when, in reality, he is emphatic that the results of his tests offer an insight which is neither fixed nor intrinsic to the biology of the individual.

One of the most vitriolic and contested applications of this line of thought maintains that as intelligence is genetically based, different 'races' have an inherently different level of intellectual aptitude. This is a position which began with Galton – who placed Anglo-Saxons at the pinnacle of intelligence, with Africans at the lowest point – but which has been a recurrent theme in the investigational literature on intelligence ever since. Most notable in this canon are the works of Yerkes (1914), Jensen (among others Rushton and Jensen, 2005) and Herrnstein and Murray (1996). This position has, however, also attracted significant critique. Some of this relates to the generally problematic nature of intelligence and of the problems of measuring it in an unbiased way (discussed further, below). Elsewhere, critique has focused on the impossibility of separating out the impacts of genetics from nurture and from poverty and other environmental factors. Even if intelligence has a biological foundation, this biology may be impacted by diet, living conditions and so on. Finally, critics (of which Gould is perhaps the most prominent) have questioned the meaningfulness of the term *race*. They highlight as much genetic diversity within 'races' as between them and claim that most diversity stems from culture rather than nature.

The critical turn on intelligence

As implied at the close of the previous section, the past half century has seen a gradually growing critical turn over the nature of intelligence, a rising debate over its nature, reality and extent. Within this debate, it is possible to discern two separate dimensions. The first relates to the methodological problems of measuring 'pure' intelligence. This goes beyond the problem of separating nature and nurture – though this is important in itself – instead implicating the problems of measuring the *capacity* to learn rather than the *content* of learning. At the most basic level, the key problem here is that IQ is generally measured through a pen-and-paper test and, as a result, the individual's level of literacy always obscures underlying intelligence (for an account of the skewing effects, see Gould, 1982).

Beyond literacy, however, is a further level of learning. Individual questions often draw unwittingly on a particular cultural context or viewpoint; they might, for instance, use names which are specific to a social group or reference experiences more familiar to one demographic than another. In this respect, even the use of imagery as a basis for the tests is skewed by culturally specific meanings and familiarities. As such, tests suffer from a cultural bias – often towards the white, middle-class authors of the IQ tests. In this respect, a group of critics of the view that intelligence is genetically determined by race have produced tests which are intentionally biased towards minority ethnicities (Dove, 1971; Williams, 1972). When such tests are administered, the differences among ethnic groups are reversed, with white middle-class respondents scoring significantly lower than their counterparts.

A second layer of critique is focused specifically on the problematic nature of intelligence as a concept. The conventional model of intellect holds it as an intrinsic and fixed variable. As such, there is a sense that intelligence is fundamentally unchanging throughout life or on a day-to-day basis; while the content of our learning may increase, our ability to think and understand may not (again, this is a point with which Binet would have disagreed). Such a stance, however, neglects to account for the ways in which logical reasoning and other skills at the core of 'intelligence' might be affected by practice. This assumption is also reflected in IQ tests, which imply a stable quantum of intellect measurable by a one-off test, the result of which might yet be influenced by an array of situational factors – illness, mood, time of day, even weather conditions.

A second line of argument in this theme questions the transcendental and foundational status given to intelligence. As we saw earlier, there has been debate over whether general intelligence underpins or is composed of other specific competencies; but within this debate there remains a fundamental commitment that it can be described as a singular property. Other theorists have, however, questioned whether general intelligence is a necessary variable and whether its existence has more to do with the imposition of an overarching property than with a genuinely occurring facet of human psychology. The most prominent of these critics is the American psychologist Howard Gardner (a former pupil of Jerome Bruner), who proposes (1983; 1993) that we should abandon the quest for a unified single characteristic and instead embrace the range of distinct **multiple intelligences** with which we are left. Initially, Gardner tentatively proposed seven forms that intelligence might take.

- **Logical-mathematical intelligence** underpins our ability to systematically analyse, to reason progressively and to investigate empirically on the basis of observation, noting patterns and making deductions.
- **Linguistic intelligence** relates to spoken and written language, whether in comprehension, acquisition (of other languages) or manipulation of words to fit ones own purposes.
- **Musical intelligence** is an affinity, whether in performance or appreciation, for pitches, rhythms and tones and for the arrangement of these properties.
- **Bodily-kinaesthetic intelligence** involves a mastery of one's own body in space at various different scales, from the delicate fine-motor skills of a watchmaker to the more grand-scale use of body in the dancer or football player.
- **Spatial intelligence** is related to perception of and understanding of the dimensions and layout of the immediate and wide environment and of navigation and negotiation within it.
- **Interpersonal intelligence** is connected to the individual's skills at empathy – understanding the needs and intentions of others – and at using this understanding to work productively within a group.
- **Intrapersonal intelligence** is self-understanding, an awareness of what makes oneself tick in terms of personal desires and fears, and the conscious management of these dimensions.

Viewed through the lens of multiple intelligences, the concept of general intelligence seems reductive, expressing as it does only one particular facet of human cognition (the first two of Gardner's forms). Such a lens also brings together the value judgements at the core of conventional views of intelligence, which privilege traditionally academic ways of thinking above all other forms of human activity. Later in his career, Gardner elaborated his model even further, adding to it categories of naturalistic, spiritual, existential and moral intelligence, though in these, he was more tentative in his conclusions.

Gardner's proposals are important, particularly in the challenge that they pose to more traditional models of intelligence. They are, however, not without their own criticisms. Many of these are focused on the seemingly arbitrary nature of the typology and the lack of empirical evidence in support of Gardner's proposals. Equally, though, there is a bipolar critique of Gardner's concept of multiple intelligence. On one hand, traditional advocates of general intelligence question whether the classifications might be reduced to more fundamental underlying factors; for instance, music might be underpinned by the same understanding of order and patterning as mathematics. Elsewhere, more radical critics (e.g. Klein, 1997) maintain that Gardner does not go far enough in deconstructing intelligence. While his model accounts for a wider variety of forms of ability, it is still fundamentally reductive; after all, if there are seven or nine intelligences, why not twelve or twenty or two hundred? It thus obscures some of the complexities inherent to cognition. Regardless of this and other critiques, however, Gardner's proposals are important challenges to thinking about intelligence and have been particularly influential in the shift from a focus on intelligence to one more concerned with learning style – the area to which the discussion now shifts.

Stop, Think, Do

In light of the critique of intelligence given so far, try to devise a more neutral concept and measurement.

Learning style

In the mid-1960s and early 1970s, educational policy and practice in Britain took a very definite turn away from the concept of intelligence and the perceived elitism in the educational policies that it inspired. The comprehensive movement – which educated all children together – was gaining momentum and with it a commitment to (if not an actualization of) a more egalitarian system of schooling. Within this more democratic ideal, though, lay an uncomfortable truth: that not all children were the same in their capacities and capabilities. A new language was needed to express this diversity without returning to the hierarchal implications of intelligence. Such a language – influenced by a new focus in psychometrics pioneered by the Myers-Briggs Type Indicator™ (Myers, 1962) – was provided by couching learning in the context of personality. This refocus allowed diversity to be expressed, not in terms of absolute scores of ability, but in learning 'preferences' and 'styles', with an implication that while differences were present, it was not necessary to impose value judgements on their relative worth.

Stop, Think, Do

Think about the notion of learning style. Identify as many different dimensions as you can through which people's preferences for learning might be distinguished (for instance, group vs. individual work).

The VARK inventory

A huge range of models, or 'inventories', of learning style have been proposed between the 1970s and the present day – some more sophisticated than others, some more popularly adopted. One model in particular, however, has attained a dominant status in educational discourse, in Britain at least, to the extent that it is often used synonymously with 'learning style', almost in denial of the existence of competing models. Fleming's (2001) VARK inventory is therefore pervasive in schools and classrooms, within government policies and teacher-training courses, as the only potential method of conceptualizing and describing learning style.

The name of this model refers to the four different learning 'styles' it describes; focusing on learners' preferences in the medium through which information is presented to them.

- **Visual learners** need to see information in order to process it; they learn particularly well when concepts are presented through diagrams, maps and pictures.
- **Auditory learners** process information more effectively when they hear it; they thus learn most effectively in traditional lecture formats and in discursive contexts such as group work or role play.
- **Read/write learners** prefer pen-and-paper work – learning from textbooks, writing essays and making revision notes.
- **Kinaesthetic learners** have a preference for physical activity and learning by doing. For these individuals, information is best encountered in tactile ways and through application in real-world activity.

The popularity of the VARK inventory is easily accounted for: it offers an accessible typology which does not make excessive use of complex theoretical or technical terminology. It also suggests tangible and easily deployed pedagogical implications. Having identified pupils who prefer kinaesthetic approaches, for instance, the teacher can begin to devise hands-on activities to maximize learning. It might be argued, though, that enthusiasm for the approach has overwhelmed a critical impulse which might have tempered its wholehearted adoption. It is relevant here, then, to consider some of the problems of the VARK inventory, as these reveal issues which are resonant in learning styles as a whole.

A particularly important criticism of the VARK inventory is that it is reductionist on two levels. On one hand, this relates to its unidimensional definition of learning style, focusing exclusively on the way in which information is presented to the learner. In doing so, the approach neglects to attend to a whole plethora of other factors: preferences concerning group and individual work, guidance and discovery, emotional and rational engagements and so on. The second layer of reductionism is in the number of styles possible, with each and every individual assigned to just one of four possible categories. More sophisticated applications of the VARK inventory allow some degree of nuance in their diagnoses – for instance, recognizing that there are 'extreme' auditory learners and those for whom the preference is less important – and allow for multimodal categories, in recognizing, for instance, that a person might lie on the boundary between read-write and auditory learning. Fundamentally, though every individual is categorized as lying somewhere within the same four fundamental categories.

A second problem with the VARK inventory is that it tends towards a deterministic conceptualization of learning style. It implies, for instance, that its diagnoses are transcendental – underpinning *all* learning with which the individual engages. It does not, therefore, account for the perfectly feasible possibility that an individual might have different learning styles in different activities or on different days or at different times within a day. Furthermore, the approach implies a degree of stability in learning style – for instance, that visual learners will remain visual learners throughout their lives.

A third related problem stems from the way in which the VARK inventory tends to be applied within classroom contexts. There is a suggestion that teachers should diagnose learning styles and then cater for those styles in their classes by giving appropriate tasks to each group of learners. Such an approach is, however, problematic on two levels. First, the amount of information which can be given to read/write learners is vastly different to that which can be covered through kinaesthetic tasks. There is, then, a real risk that children might be accidentally denied access to knowledge and understanding as a result of 'meeting their learning style'. The second tension is that in catering for a particular learning style, children are not challenged to shift that style to become more flexible and rounded learners. In respect to this layer of critique there is, of course, a pragmatic response: lessons should be planned in such a way as to ensure that all children are given a mixture of visual, auditory, read/write and kinaesthetic learning so as to both challenge preference and cater for it. In doing so, though, it remains important to be mindful of the practical challenges of the inventory and to recognize its serious theoretical flaws.

Learning style and hemispheric lateralization

Alongside the VARK inventory, a second dominant strand in the discourse of learning style focuses on the role of neurophysiology – brain structure – in determining learning style. Indeed, Fleming's model was itself influenced by earlier work which explored the different ways (called sensory modalities) in which the brain represented and encoded information in language, sound, movement and so on. An alternative branch of this approach begins with **hemispheric lateralization**, the observation that the brain is split into two hemispheres, left and right, each performing different functions. Thus, variations in individual learning style might be accounted for through dominance in one or other of these hemispheres and thus a preference for its particular functions.

The most popular understanding of hemispheric dominance is that the left side governs rational thought, while the right is responsible for creativity. Many brain-based learning-style approaches take this as a starting point; most notably, Barbara Vitale (1985) argues that two forms of preference emerge from hemispheric dominance. The first relates to the individual's 'consciousness', or preference in how he or she thinks about things. In this respect, left-dominant individuals, according to Vitale, prefer to think in linear, logical ways; they begin with individual components of an idea and gradually build up to the 'big picture'. Right-dominant learners, in contrast, are more likely to prefer holistic thinking; they begin with the big picture and pick it apart in random and intuitive ways in order to isolate its component parts. The second of Vitale's dimensions of learning style concerns the types of 'skill' with which individuals have particular aptitude – that is, the things that they can do rather than the ways that they can think. Left-dominant individuals, she argues, are more skilled with language, whether written or spoken, in following instructions, in locating details and facts. Those who are right dominant are more attuned to spatial relationships (patterns and shapes), to creativity, to feelings and emotions.

The reference made to biology in approaches such as Vitale's gives them an apparent scientific basis. It is, however, worth exercising critical caution in this respect. While the terminology used by these models lends them a degree of apparent credibility, the actual empirical evidence in support of them is less than authoritative. On one hand, there is certainly neurophysiological evidence in support of hemispherical lateralization in relation to macro functions. Roger Sperry (1968), for instance, successfully demonstrated that the right side of the brain controlled the left side of the body and vice versa – a phenomenon called contralateral control – and that vocalization of language was controlled by a specific hemisphere. There is also some tentative evolutionary theory (Shlain, 1999) which argues that preferences for holistic or linear thinking might be a hangover from early human socialization and the conditions of hunters and gatherers, who needed a sensitivity to the big picture and to the details of their environment.

Elsewhere, however, the majority of biological evidence suggests that neurophysiology is vastly oversimplified in models of learning style which emphasize left or right dominance. Rather, logic and other complex functions are realized through the interplay of many different regions of the brain (within and across hemispheres) which are activated in only semi-predictable ways. Even if, therefore, it were possible to properly understand the regions of the brain responsible for different skills and aptitudes, applying these to the more complex and multifaceted ecology of the classroom would be far from straightforward.

The temptation of a scientized model of learning style also detracts from more fundamental theoretical problems. The approach is heavily deterministic; in locating learning styles in the physical structure of the brain, it leaves little space to accommodate the notion that such styles can change and no real role for the individual as an autonomous and self-directed agent in learning. The approach is also fundamentally reductionist; both in its identification of the determinants of behaviour (biology, without other influences) and in the number of possible styles it allows. In Vitale's model, for instance, individuals are either left or right dominant – a typology which seems to obscure the richness and diversity that learning preference might take.

Kolb's typology

While VARK and brain-based approaches to learning style, despite all their faults, have attained dominance in educational practice, they do not enjoy the same status in academic treatments of education. In this respect, a more successful model can be found in that proposed by David Kolb's (1984) experiential learning theory (Figure 3.1). Where the VARK approach implicates just one dimension of learning style (medium of presentation), Kolb's approach suggests that we focus on two. The first of these – the **perceptual continuum** – relates to the way in which individuals approach and encounter information and tasks. On one extreme of this continuum is a preference for **concrete experience** – in which ideas are encountered in contexts which are meaningful to the individual, either through example or application (such as the use of light bulbs and batteries to illustrate electricity) or through an appeal to feelings (for instance, understanding the Holocaust through empathy-generating case studies). At the other extreme of the continuum is a preference for **abstract conceptualization** – encountering information in theoretical terms. Electricity, in this respect, might be introduced in relation to underlying atomic theory, while the Holocaust might be conceptualized in terms of the historical forces that shaped it.

The second of Kolb's dimensions of learning style, the **processing continuum**, describes the way in which individuals transform and personalize experiences. Here again there are two extremes. At one is **reflective observation**, denoting individuals who prefer to sit back and think about experiences in order to make sense of them; at the other, **active experimentation** prefers a more hands-on, trial-and-error approach to learning. In learning about electricity, then, individuals with a preference for the first of these dimensions learn more effectively when ideas are demonstrated to them, whereas the latter would learn more effectively if given circuits to play with. Kolb argues that preferences across these two dimensions combine to create four distinct styles of learner, each with particular strengths.

- **Accommodators** (concrete experience and active experimentation) are particularly good hands-on and 'in the moment'. Thus, they are able to solve problems by drawing on their intuition and are comfortable taking risks based on the available information.
- **Divergers** (concrete experience and reflective observation) are also happy in the moment, though their strengths tend more towards imagination and perspective taking. They are good at generating lots of competing ideas.
- **Assimilators** (abstract conceptualization and reflective observation) are particularly good at theorizing – at taking stock of available evidence and integrating it into logical and coherent models.

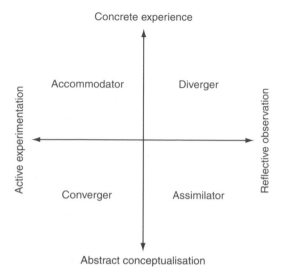

Figure 3.1

- **Convergers** (abstract conceptualization and active experimentation) are strong in the practical deployment of ideas – taking theoretical models and ideas and putting them into practice in real-life contexts.

Compared to the VARK inventory, Kolb's model of learning style is significantly less reductive. On one hand, this is because it implicates two separate dimensions of style and focuses on the internal psychology of individuals rather than simply on mode of presentation. The model is also more accommodating of differences within learning styles. While there are four key categories, the use of continuums to diagnose them allows for different levels of extremes. Kolb's model is also less deterministic than both the VARK and brain-based approaches. While he maintains that individuals have a tendency towards one of these styles – and that this gives them particular preferences and aptitudes – nothing is fixed in his model. Rather than being innate, learning style is a product of habit and is capable of being changed. Indeed, Kolb actively maintains that individuals should be challenged to shift their learning style, given that the most effective learners are balanced and equally comfortable with concrete experience, abstract conceptualization, reflective observation and active experimentation. In making this assertion, Kolb situates learning style in a broader model (which he calls **experiential learning theory**) that envisages all learning as consisting of an ongoing cycle, which begins with experience and reflection on that experience, continues through the introduction of more generalized theoretical models (abstract conceptualization) and experimentation with these models to apply them to new contexts. There are here echoes of some of the other cognitive theories explored in Chapter 1, notably Ausubel's assertion that learning starts with what the learner already knows and Bruner's model of the spiral curriculum. Other theorists have used Kolb's learning cycle as the basis of concrete pedagogies. Most notably, McCarthy (1980) devised the 4Mat system, which advises that teachers plan lessons so that they move through each of the four forms of learning, thus ensuring that learning styles are both catered for and challenged.

This model, too, is not without criticism. On one hand, empirical support for the model is weak, and there is a convenient correspondence between Kolb's model of learning and his inventory of style, often to the extent that the reader is asked to accept the existence of the former as justification of the latter. Further, while the model is significantly less reductionist than other, simpler approaches, it still fundamentally defines learning style as a two-dimensional phenomenon and therefore ignores other important factors. Other approaches have attempted to address this problem by appending additional dimensions to their inventories, and it is with these models that we finish this discussion.

Stop, Think, Do

Review the key dimensions and styles of the inventories covered so far. Reflect on how your learning style might relate to them. Reflect on the extent to which your learning style changes in different contexts and times. Can you really be described as having one learning style?

Multidimensional models of learning style

Although VARK is a dominant approach in educational practice and Kolb enjoys dominance in education theory, a range of additional approaches to learning style has attempted to provide a more holistic inventory. By drawing on multiple dimensions of style, they attempt to avoid some of the problems of reductionism associated with simpler approaches and to provide a diagnosis which is more sensitive to the diversity of learners (and thus yield implications which are more effective in practice). One well-known form of this inventory is that provided by Dunn and Dunn (2000): a model composed of five separate dimensions, each of which in turn is made up of a number of subfactors (21 in all).

- **Environmental preference** relates to the learners' effectiveness with different levels of light, sound and temperature in the preferred seating arrangement.
- **Emotional factors** are linked to the individuals' motivation, persistence (their need to complete one task before beginning another) and responsibility and to the degree of structure they need in tasks in order to feel comfortable.
- **Sociological preferences** are linked to the individuals' relationships with others during learning. The simplest subdimension, here, is whether the individual is more comfortable working in isolation or with others. There are, however, subtler dimensions: whether, for instance, they need an authority figure or prefer collegial learning and whether they need routine in these relationships.
- **Physiological needs** relate to the individuals' biological states and functioning. One dimension here is the perceptual strand (auditory, visual, tactile or kinaesthetic), together with their energy levels at different points in the day and their need for mobility or stillness.
- **Psychological needs** are focused on the individuals' internal processing of information. On one hand, this involves the kinds of left- and right-hemisphere preferences identified by Vitale. In addition, Dunn and Dunn implicate a separate set of preferences for global (or holistic) and analytic (or linear) learners and for impulsive or reflective learning.

A similar multidimensional model is proposed by Curry (1983), who suggests that we imagine learning style as being like an onion – composed of layers, each distinct but interrelated, and each with its own relative level of stability.

- **Instructional preference** forms the outermost layer. It relates to those factors which surround learning but which are external to the learner. These preferences relate, for instance, to how the learner prefers teachers to behave, together with environmental factors (temperature, noise levels, etc.) and preferences about the way in which material is presented to them (the VARK typology would most neatly fit within this layer). Curry argues that as this layer is on the 'surface', it is influenced by a plethora of contextual variables (such as the subject, teacher and parental expectations), and it is thus the least stable and most susceptible to fluctuation and change on both a day-to-day basis and throughout life.

- **Informational processing style** forms the middle layer of Curry's model and relates to the strategies used to process and make sense of information once it has been presented. The dimensions identified by Kolb largely fit within this layer; they include preferences of the 'heart over mind' type (such as those found in the perceptual continuum). This layer is more stable than instructional preference, yet it is still subject to fluctuation and change – by being actively challenged by teachers, for instance.
- **Cognitive personality style** is the final, innermost layer of Curry's model. It is heavily linked to the individual's personality and is made up of psychometric traits such as intelligence, introversion/extroversion and the kinds of 'consciousness' featured in Vitale's model. Personality, in this model, is formed during early experience, but it quickly becomes stable and relatively unchanging.

In Curry's model, therefore, dimensions of learning style become more fixed and stable in the core layers and more transient and changing in the outer layers. There is also a sense that the inner layers influence those which surround them. To illustrate: an individual who tends towards introversion (a feature of cognitive personality style) is unlikely to enjoy role play (which is related to instructional preference).

The key advantage of the models provided by Curry and by Dunn and Dunn is that they provide a more holistic sense of learning and a set of inventories that accommodate more of the diversity of learners found in the population. Further, there is a greater sense of variability in these approaches, and they can more easily accommodate a sense that facets of individuals' learning style might shift over time and across contexts. Inherent to this advantage is, however, a fundamental problem: as the construction of learning style becomes more fragmented and multiple – and as it becomes less stable and predictable – it also becomes less easily applicable to real-life classroom settings. Given a set of four styles – visual, auditory, kinaesthetic and read/write, for instance – teachers can happily adjust their practice in concrete ways to better meet the needs of learners. Faced with 21 variables (as in the case of Dunn and Dunn's model) which are never stable and fixed, the task becomes more daunting.

It could be argued, then, that models of learning style are caught within a fundamental tension; on one hand, in order to be applicable, they need to have an element of stability and simplicity. If, however, the concern is with accuracy and the degree to which such models reflect the detail and diversity of how people *actually* learn in real-life contexts, then it is necessary to include a degree of flexibility and fluidity in diagnosis. It is also necessary to recognize the multidimensional nature of both learning and personality and the complex interplays of the various facets of each. Ultimately, this layering of dimensions multiplies the number of possible diagnoses exponentially until ultimately we end up with an inventory which diagnoses every learner as having a distinct style – which, possibly, is the most accurate reflection of reality.

Critical perspectives on learning style

Before concluding this section, it is worth noting that while the term *learning style* is still dominant in educational theory and practice, recent years have seen a growing discontent with the construct and an increasingly critical voice directed at its principles. A large proportion of this critique stems from the lack of empirical evidence in support of the existence of learning style as a genuine feature of human psychology or for the impact of catering for such styles on the effectiveness and quality of learning. Indeed, a range of theorists have been overtly critical of the concept's theoretical basis, measurement and implications. Coffield et al. (2004), for instance, reviewed the 13 most prevalent inventories in terms of their theoretical basis and method of measurement and the empirical work which had been conducted around them. Having found little to validate the claims of any of the dominant models, they concluded that the impact of adapting teaching practice to cater for learning style was highly questionable.

Given this lack of empirical support, it seems that the success of learning styles in achieving a hold on educational discourse marks the degree to which such models have been promoted (often by commercial companies, in specially retailed packages). They also feature an enticing claim: that they offer a 'golden bullet' with which to address diverse needs and improve the educational attainment of all learners. This is obviously an offer which appeals to the good intentions of educations and policymakers alike. Coffield and his colleagues, however, advise caution in this respect; what appears to be a meeting of individual needs might, in equal measure, be seen as a process of labelling, of boxing learners into a particular set of experiences based on a diagnosis with no real methodological or theoretical foundation. The researchers do, however, offer some positive words on learning style, recognizing that the models are useful when used as devices for thinking. By combining all of the different types of learning style, we begin to appreciate the multi-faceted and complex nature of the ways in which individual differences mediate learning. By engaging with this understanding across educational practice – rather than medically 'diagnosing' learners as particular types – it is possible to foster a more responsive and sensitive educative practice.

Conclusions

In this section, then, we have considered two major types of educational and psychological discourse on individual variables in the learning process: the areas of intelligence and learning style. It is perhaps worth finishing with two observations on the discussion. First, both concepts are social constructs – and situating them in a historical context helps to expose this fact. Thus, it becomes apparent that the popularization of each concept is embedded, in part at least, in the social and political climate of the time. Intelligence, for instance, emerged in an era buoyed by a new-found interest in evolutionary biology and natural selection, and it was popularized in a political climate which emphasized 'appropriate' education and within a social context which was heavily hierarchical and class based. The notion of intelligence, then, provided some justification for the stratification of educational experience and of life chances of individuals. It supported the view, for instance, that the middle and upper classes had received a better education because of – and had had a higher social status conferred upon them as a product of – their superior intelligence.

The discourse of learning styles, in contrast, emerged in a very different social and political climate. The post-war era had seen a backlash against the class system which came to a head in the liberalization of the 1960s; the result was a persistent call for egalitarianism and equality in society. This was pushed by the progressive movement in education during the 1970s, which attempted to provide all members of society with the same standard of education. Learning styles, in this context, were appealing because they offered a way of recognizing difference without creating an associated hierarchy. The construct continued to maintain influence throughout the 1980s and 1990s and into the new century on the back of a political discourse of 'standards' (on the right wing of politics) and 'equality of opportunity' (on the left), as they offered a pedagogical suggestion that might narrow the differences in achievement across different social groups.

The second observation is that these debates are complicated by the multiple stakeholders involved in them. On one hand, educators and policymakers seek meaningful and practical methods of describing and responding to difference among learners, while psychologists and others with a theoretical interest in education seek instead the most accurate method of describing and measuring these complex differences. It is easy to disregard one side of this tension or the other, but the fundamental problem is that both need to be addressed. There is little point in being able to describe differences among learners without responding to them or in responding to perceived differences if they have no basis in reality. It may, of course, be the case that intelligence or one of the myriad models of learning style offer a method of achieving this – or at least a framework through which to better appreciate that those differences exist. Equally, though, it may be that these constructs are counterproductive, in that they obscure the true diversity of difference among learners, and that, without them, teachers may be more able to appreciate and respond to these differences at the level of each unique individual.

Key questions

- How has the conceptual construct of intelligence evolved? Which key theorists and thinkers have contributed to the process?
- How have the concepts of intelligence and IQ influenced educational policy, practice and provision?
- What controversies and criticisms have surrounded the definition and use of intelligence?
- How has the concept of learning style attempted to provide an alternative framework to that of intelligence?
- What are the different proposed models of learning style?
- What tensions underpin models of learning style? To which criticisms have these models been subjected?
- How might the concepts of learning style and intelligence be situated in a political and historical context?

Further reading

Coffield, F., D. Moseley, E. Hall and K. Ecclestone (2004). *Learning Styles and Pedagogy in post-16 Learning: A Systematic and Critical Review*. London: Learning and Skills Research Centre.

Dunn, R. (2000). 'Learning styles: Theory, research and practice'. *National Forum of Applied Educational Research Journal*, 13, 3–22.

Gardner, H. (1993). *Multiple Intelligences: The Theory in Practice*. New York: Basic Books.

Gould, S. (1982). 'A nation of morons'. *New Scientist*, 349.

—(1996). *The Mismeasure of Man*. New York: Norton.

Herrnstein, R., and C. Murray (1996). *The Bell Curve: Intelligence and Class Structure in American Life*. London: Simon and Schuster.

Kolb, D. 1984. *Experiential Learning*. Englewood Cliffs, NJ: Prentice Hall.

Contexts of Curriculum 4

So far in this text our focus has been very broadly on learning – on examining various competing perspectives on the process and experiences through which individuals might come to understand – and in the previous chapter, specifically on the ways in which variation in this process among individuals might be explained. In this chapter and in those which follow it, we shift our focus from the hows of learning to the whats. Thus, our central concern here is with the curriculum, the content of learning which occurs in any educational setting. In considering curriculum, it is sometimes difficult to distance oneself from conventions – that, for instance, the school day should be composed of subjects and that these subjects should include science, maths, English, history and so on. A common strand that underpins this second segment of the text maintains, however, that the programme of learning which occurs in educational institutions should be treated not as a natural given but as a social construct. Thus, we maintain that the curriculum can never be studied in isolation from the society that produces it.

Two distinct dimensions might be identified in this; on one hand, the curriculum is based on a broader system of knowledge, which has been collectively accumulated by society – a process which necessarily involves the validation of some ways of knowing and the marginalization of others. Further, the curriculum itself draws on only a limited subset of these understandings, and this selection involves judgements as to what is most important and worthwhile within society's knowledge system, based on assumptions of what purposes that curriculum is intended to serve.

The function of this chapter, then, is to begin to equip the reader with some mechanisms through which to 'denormalize' the curriculum, to see it as something which is ideologically and conceptually contested. Doing so will help the reader to begin to recognize the ways in which convention has been established through social and historical construction. Here we do this by considering some of the philosophical debates which underpin curriculum and which define competing 'paradigms' that govern the approach to designing programmes of learning. We then consider the historical processes though which the curriculum, in its current incarnation in the United Kingdom, has been built and shaped (connecting together philosophical and political ideology). In later chapters, we adopt a more explicitly sociological lens to consider the influence of power and social differentiation in shaping the programme of learning which occurs in schools.

> ### Stop, Think, Do
>
> Reflect on the curriculum as it currently is; attempt to identify some of the conventions and assumptions that underpin it. Try to imagine an alternative way of organizing educational experiences, a way completely different to these conventions. Consider the extent to which the current curriculum is the natural and unchallengeable way of organizing learning.

Philosophical contexts

As introduced above, it is impossible to separate curriculum from the society which constructs it and from the ends which that society wishes it to meet. The earliest treatises on knowledge and curriculum, those of the ancient Greek philosophers, were sensitive to these points. Aristotle began his analysis of the nature of knowledge by considering how it was exercised by people in the wider society (Aristotle, 2000). He identified three distinct forms of understanding, which he saw as distinct strands of knowledge and thus the foundations of the curriculum:

- The **theoretical** form, which is concerned with knowledge for its own sake. Here learning is its own reward in terms of space to think and contemplate and to appreciate the elegance of the thinking that has already occurred among others. In the society of which Aristotle was a member, this was the remit of the philosophers.
- The **productive** form, which is focused on using knowledge to make things. This might have involved the acquisition and exercise of a vocational skill; for instance, the knowledge that an ironmonger might need to ply his trade. Equally, though, Aristotle uses this form to refer to artistic production. So the form's range extended from the artisan trades to the uses of language among poets.
- The **practical** form, which is easily confused with the productive, although its focus is distinct in referring to the use of knowledge to make judgements rather than to produce artefacts. Aristotle saw this form as being exercised by governors and judges, as well as in the ethical decisions of everyday people. A key distinction here is that the productive exercise of knowledge begins with a plan or intent about an end product, while the practical exercise begins with an appraisal of a situation.

The influence of Aristotle's distinction between these three forms of knowledge is significant, and the division has echoed through the philosophy of curriculum ever since. Thus, while there has been complicated interplay of the three forms, one major strand of debate within curriculum theory has related to balancing several factors: theoretical content, the ability to do things practically, and the extent to which learners should be developed as thinkers and judgers. In turn, this tension of balance has inspired three distinct traditions of curriculum design, and it is to these to which we now turn our attention.

The liberal tradition

For some curriculum theorists, the purpose of education is to produce rounded individuals, with experience of the full range of ways in which society thinks and expresses itself. In this, the tradition of liberal education, learners should therefore be immersed in the full spectrum of knowledge areas and understandings which are deemed central to their particular culture – the arts, the sciences, the humanities and so on. For this tradition, learning is its own end and reward – it does not have or require external justification – and it thus derives most directly from the Aristotelian notion of theoretical knowledge. In designing a curriculum, the focus of this tradition is, therefore, with carefully designing a **syllabus** that draws on a sample of content which exposes learners to a full array of subject areas and a canon of 'big thinkers' who have contributed to those areas.

The philosophical challenge that faces liberal curriculum designers is in determining *what* learning best represents the range of different forms of knowledge drawn upon by society. Without an understanding of this, it is impossible to construct a rounded programme of learning. One of the best-known attempts to answer this was provided by Paul Hirst (Hirst and Peters, 1970). His starting point was the assertion of 'a basic philosophical truth about the nature of knowledge that, whether we like it or not, knowledge is differentiated into distinct forms or disciplines.' From this point, Hirst set out to reduce all types of human knowledge to basic categories which were fundamentally distinct from one another in terms of their logics, languages and methodologies – what he called, the 'irreducible forms' of knowledge. He settled, eventually, on seven of these categories: mathematics, physical science, human science, history, religion, literature and art, philosophy and morality. Hirst's call was that a liberal education should develop thinking balanced across these areas – though not necessarily by including corresponding subjects. Rather, the logics of different forms can be combined to create fields of knowledge; for instance, geography draws on aspects of both the physical and human sciences, while 'citizenship' might be seen to be based on the historical, moral and human sciences.

The liberal tradition in curriculum design has clear positive sentiments. Most importantly, it seeks to provide all learners – regardless of social background or apparent ability – with the same set of opportunities, the same experience of a broad and rounded syllabus of understanding. It consequently rallies against specialization occurring too early in an individual's educational career, with its associated risks that learners might be labelled with particular academic and vocational destinies before they have fully developed. Indeed, in the United States, where the tradition of liberal education is more notably embedded, learners are discouraged from overspecialization even in higher education – hence, the conventions of 'major' and 'minor' concentrations in one's degree work.

Further, in maintaining a focus on the production of rounded individuals, the liberal tradition of curriculum is resistant to reductive tendencies in education. On one hand, this is related to content – as noted above, curriculum planners in this tradition strive for a programme which is diverse in its coverage. This also extends, however, to purposes of education. For a liberal educator, the benefits of learning cannot be reduced to simple outcomes or 'capabilities'; the process of education is also about the formation of character, interest, moral and ethical thought and so on. The tradition has, as its template and aim, an image of the Renaissance man (an individual such as Leonardo da Vinci), fundamentally defined by manifold interests in a range of activities.

The liberal tradition has generated several key dimensions of critique, however. It could be argued, for instance, that the emphasis on a broad syllabus in the approach ultimately equates to a large amount of pointless learning. This argument relates to the significance and relevance of content to the learners themselves, in terms of their particular concerns and interests, their abilities and capacities. There is consequently a risk that large numbers of students, beyond those with a narrowly 'academic' interest and ability, will become marginalized or outright bored by their educational experience and thus become disengaged from the process. From an alternative perspective, therefore, the entitlement of pupils to a broad curriculum could be seen as forcing learners to engage with content which holds little or no interest to them.

The relevance of the content of liberal curricula can also be questioned in a broader context. As the key guiding principle of the tradition lies in the syllabus, little attention is given to the external applicability or usefulness of learning in, for example, the workplace. In short, learners who have experienced a liberal curriculum may leave with a broad range of intellectual experiences but without an ability to actually *do* anything with them. Detractors at the extreme of this set of critics have argued that the emphasis on theoretical content in the liberal tradition excludes the development of key skills needed by business and industry and thus disables education from responding to the needs of the economy. In turn, advocates of liberal education maintain that such responsiveness occupies only a tiny subset of the much broader and more important aims of education.

A second layer of critique of the liberal approach to curriculum centres on the nature of the canon on which the syllabus is based. On one hand, this is a philosophical problem, and attempts, such as Hirst's, to isolate fundamentally discrete and irreducible forms of knowledge have attracted substantial criticism (e.g. Schilling, 1986; Warnock, 1977). On one hand, this is because the categories on which they draw are too 'neat', remain open to intermixing and are based on non-specific and interchangeable uses of terms such as 'knowledge', 'understanding' and 'experience'. Thus, the reduced forms of knowledge seem arbitrary; they open endless debates about the logical home of particular ideas.

Further, while Hirst and like-minded theorists contend that their selection of subject domains and content is based on rational, logical and detached judgement, other have argued that – in reality – issues of power are always embroiled in what constitutes legitimate content. On one level, this is because what constitutes valid 'truth' within society's knowledge system (and on which the curriculum is based) shifts over time. Michel Foucault (2001; 1979; 1969), for instance, has documented the ways in which the dominant *episteme* of society (the agency with the greatest claim to the truth) has shifted throughout history – from, for instance, religion to science – and the impacts that this has had on what constitutes truth more broadly in society.

Beyond this broader construction of knowledge, commentators have documented the ways in which the process of selection of content for inclusion in the curriculum challenges its claims to be objective and neutral. They argue that it inevitably develops a bias towards the interests and concerns of the social groups with the most power to influence it. In the language of Pierre Bourdieu (Bourdieu and Passeron, 1973; Bourdieu, 1986), the curriculum thus becomes colonized by the cultural capital of white middle-class men – emphasizing so-called high culture (theatre, conventional literature, etc.) over popular forms, not because of its inherent importance to society but because it is preferred by those with greater social power and influence. In turn, this creates a bias in achievement; those learners who share this social background – and are thus more familiar with the cultural capital which is valued in the curriculum – are at an advantage (hence, the use of the term 'capital' is intentional, as culture has relative 'value' which can be 'cashed in' within the appropriate context).

As a consequence of these processes, critics have noted that non-dominant cultures are systematically excluded from the curriculum. On one hand, this might relate directly to activities which are outside the mainstream (rap, for instance, as a form of literature). Equally, though, this might relate to distortions within this mainstream, which systematically rewrite history to downplay the contributions of other cultures and peoples. George Gheverghese Joseph (2000), for instance, has presented a historical account of mathematics (an apparently apolitical and objective field of knowledge), noting that the usual tale of the subject traces its origins to Greece and thus western Europe. This, he argues, systematically sidelines the legacy and contribution of earlier non-Western civilizations, from which a large segment of the subject is drawn.

A final strand of critique of the liberal tradition of curriculum debate relates to the way in which learners are encouraged to engage with the syllabus. While the approach tends to use language emphasizing the development of learners as independent, rational thinkers, in reality the canon on which the curriculum is based tends to be treated as relatively fixed and sacred. Thus, learners are not encouraged to disagree with the ideas established as dogma in the various subject areas, and any criticality that emerges is ultimately bounded within parameters. Individuals might be encouraged, for instance, to engage in debates about the meaning and significance of aspects of a Shakespeare play, but rarely would they be encouraged to suggest that study of these plays is less legitimate than the study of a television soap opera. Similarly, the kinds of ethnocentric histories identified by George (2000) are left unchallenged.

The instrumental tradition

While the liberal tradition stems from Aristotle's theoretical knowledge, the instrumental approach is instead influenced by the productive form. Here the key measure of the curriculum is the extent to which it equips learners with the capacity to do things; in this approach knowledge is only valid if it is useful in immediate, practical ways. Thus, the emphasis in this approach to the curriculum is on the **product** of learning, both immediately and in the longer term. More extreme and more obvious applications of this tradition can be found in vocational education and training, in which the curriculum is literally oriented to enable learners to perform skills that underpin specific jobs and trades. Instrumentalism is not, however, synonymous with vocationalism; as we will explore below, it has also framed more traditionally academic curriculums. Here, the tradition manifests itself as an emphasis on 'learning objectives', which describe what a particular individual should be able to do as a result of his or her exposure to aspects of the curriculum and to the broader competencies to which these contribute (contrast this with the liberal approach, which sees engagement as an end in itself).

The instrumental tradition of curriculum grew from an emerging field of 'scientific management' (stemming from the work of Taylor, 1911) and was taken from the field of business and applied to education by thinkers such as Bobbitt (1918) and Tyler (1949). These theorists proposed a curriculum design process very different to that explored in the liberal tradition.

1. Rather than beginning with an analysis of knowledge and a sense of the syllabus transmitted to learners, the instrumental tradition starts by looking at the broader society and at the kinds of activities which learners will need to be able to perform once they have left formal education.
2. From here, curriculum planners begin to select particular competencies which they wish to develop in learners and to break these down into a series of objectives and learning outcomes.
3. It is only at this point that content (which ruled the liberal design process from the very beginning) can be selected and the curriculum populated with ideas and understandings that will facilitate the kinds of outcomes identified.

The instrumental tradition is particularly attractive to policymakers, as it offers a mechanism through which to centrally produce a tidy and well-organized curriculum. Importantly, its emphasis on outcomes brings with it an inherent measurability – useful not only in terms of examination and qualification but also in monitoring the quality of education and holding schools and teachers to account. To this end, a further layer of 'quality control' is offered by this approach to curriculum; the predictable organization of its content means that resources can be designed to support teaching and mitigate the variability of student experiences. Finally, because the model begins with an interrogation of social need and designs the curriculum from this perspective, the relevance of learning is clearer than in the liberal tradition and more responsive to shifting economic needs. Thus, for example, as ICT becomes more important in the workplace, content that develops learners' skills with these technologies can be integrated.

The instrumental tradition suffers, however, from a reductive tendency on a number of distinct levels. Most overwhelmingly, it defines the functions of education in narrow ways, often focusing on the need to meet economic and social demands. As a result, it also curtails the breadth of curriculum (a key strength of the liberal tradition), marginalizing content which does not meet these needs in direct and obvious ways. Furthermore, the instrumental approach to curriculum tends to reduce what constitutes legitimate and valid learning to those things that are pre-approved in its learning objectives. Such a stance is arguably narrow and short-sighted. On one hand, it marginalizes any incidental, or as Dewey refers to it, 'collateral' learning (1938), though such learning may have profound relevance to the learner. On the other hand, the immediacy of learning objectives neglects to account for any 'slow-burn' impacts of learning – those understandings that may gain resonance only much later in the learner's life.

There is, associated with this emphasis on outcomes and objectives, a consequent construction of what being a teacher or a learner is, a construction whose impact can be felt in the classroom. The learner is construed as passively acquiring skills and competencies, and learning is judged as successful if an assessor can tick off a series of particular behavioural outcomes. Consequently, acquiring the capacity for autonomous thought – being able to operate outside prescribed outcomes – is of secondary importance; a sense of overarching mastery can only be expressed as a competence (the sum of a series of objectives rather than something that transcends them). To illustrate, poets do more than just use words in competent ways – the goal in an instrumental approach – rather, they have a mastery over words and meanings that draws upon these skills but also transcends them.

The reduction of learning to a series of measurable objects also reduces the role of the teacher to a technical model. Thus, teachers become responsible for disseminating and delivering the curriculum according to its narrowly defined parameters. Arguably, such an approach negates (or at least de-emphasizes) the need for professional judgements among teachers; indeed, it is this that allows the approach to claim a higher level of quality control in schools. In sidelining this ability to act organically and interactively with learners, however, something of the responsiveness and pedagogic skill of teaching is also lost. All of this is magnified by the punitive tone with which the discourse of objectives is used politically:

> 'What are your objectives?' is more often asked in a tone of challenge than one of interested and helpful inquiry. The demand for objectives is a demand for justification rather than a description of ends. (Stenhouse, 1975)

This emphasis on meeting centrally defined objectives effectively in education further erodes a teacher's autonomous judgement (as attention must be given to the central curriculum), and this may have the effect of further reducing the breadth of the education. At the most severe, then, an outcome-centric curriculum might lead to 'assessment backwash' (Biggs, 1999): 'teaching to the test' in order to ensure that outcomes are met at the expense of any richness and diversity in the learners' experience. Such a process can be compounded by the learners themselves; an educational culture of measurable outcomes can lead to a feeling that learning is only worthwhile if it will consequently be tested.

The critical/process tradition

So far, then, we have explored two distinct paradigms of curriculum design; the first emphasizing the content around which the curriculum is organized, and the second focusing primarily on the outcomes and products of learning. A third distinct tradition has, however, emerged with a very different set of priorities. Here, the **process** of engagement with the curriculum is emphasized over its content and outcomes, with priority therefore given to the interactions of teacher, student and content in the classroom. The concept can seem alien, largely because it is an underutilized tradition in the British context, but can be illustrated with a simple example of a physics lesson, in which a magnetic field around a coil is fluctuated in order to induce electrical current. For a syllabus-driven liberal educator, such a session would be aimed at immersing learners in the contributions of a great thinker in physics (in this case, Faraday). In a product-oriented instrumental tradition, the aim would be more directly to enable learners to explain the specific principles of electromagnetic induction and their potential applications. A process-based model, by contrast, would be much more focused on the students' emerging experimentations with scientific models and their engagement with a set of propositions surrounding subject matter. Learners who do so leave better equipped to evaluate scientific claims themselves; in this respect, the tradition can be seen as a clear legacy of the Aristotelian notion of practical knowledge (that which underpins judgements rather than products).

The early tenets of a process-led curriculum were most clearly expressed by British educationalist Lawrence Stenhouse (1975), beginning with a definition that 'a curriculum is an attempt to communicate the essential principles and features of an educational proposal in such a form that it is open to critical scrutiny and capable of effective translation into practice'. Crucial, here, is the notion of scrutiny – the sense that classrooms should be places in which learners are encouraged to critically engage and assess notions in context. There is, according to Stenhouse, still a place for planned programmes of learning, for a need to design experiences with which students can engage. However, these programmes should be treated as proposals which 'claim to be intelligent rather than correct' (1975, 142). Further, any planned curriculum should be treated as a starting point, a stimulus from which learning can progress in unpredictable ways, guided by the emerging interests of learners.

For Stenhouse and his contemporaries, the curriculum should therefore be aimed at fostering intelligent, rational and independent *judgement* among learners. Others have, however, taken this to a more radical end. They argue that judgement is only a starting point: education should be aiming to foster critical and committed action (or praxis) in the world. Thus, the critical faculties of learners should be developed in ways that enable them to pursue a fairer and more equal world. Faced with Joseph George's observations on the ethnocentric biases in the history of mathematics, for instance, learners should be actively interrogating racist misrepresentations in this specific aspect of history, and in history more generally, in order to expose alternative realities and unrepresented voices.

There is, of course, a risk inherent to this process of committed and radical enquiry: rather than operate as autonomous and principled individuals, learners might be indoctrinated with the political views of their teachers. As a consequence (and following Freire, 1996; 2001), advocates of this critical model of curriculum maintain that it is necessary to erode the power differential that exists between teacher and student. In this model teachers become facilitators who are willing to learn from their students, to respect their voices, understandings and capacities as autonomous individuals. Conversely, students' experience and knowledge are given status equal to that of the 'official line', and they to an extent become teachers.

The advantages of the process-oriented and critical traditions in curriculum design over alternative forms are clear: they aim at producing independent and autonomous thinkers, committed to their principles. Such an aim is, of course, laudable in itself; it sets out to create an education system which is actively humanizing and nourishing, treating its learners as active agents and not passive recipients of content. Beyond this, however, are more direct and utilitarian benefits. In encouraging its learners to engage with processes and contexts rather than fixed outcomes, it has the potential to enable them to be more flexible and responsive, to independently weigh given situations in order to deploy their learning effectively.

In contrast to both the liberal and instrumental traditions, the process-led curriculum also actively encourages teachers to engage with learners as a first priority rather than as an additional aspect of practice to 'content'. Here, then, is a curriculum that can be responsive to individual interests and emerging talents and which is driven by an ongoing interaction rather than a focus on a distant end point. Arguably, then, a process-based curriculum has the potential to foster effective and practitioner-determined pedagogy – and thus a more effective quality of learning.

This strength is, however, also the key drawback of the approach, for its success pivots to a great extent on the ability of teachers to effectively facilitate it. For political agents in charge of education, then, a process-led curriculum is prohibitively risky. There is a degree of legitimacy to this concern, because it inevitably introduces a large degree of variation into the experience of learners. This could potentially mean a widening gap in achievement, and as is often the case, it is likely that schools in less 'desirable' areas would suffer as a result. Any attempt for central government to mitigate these disparities – for instance, by providing learning resources around which to structure the process of education – is likely to compromise the model, taking it closer to a product-led approach.

Even where teacher quality can be assured, the process-led curriculum, without any fixed end points, tends towards a lack of uniformity. This, in turn, introduces a further layer of critique: how does one set about designing fair and commonly applicable examinations through which to assess learning and award A levels, GCSEs and the like? An extreme version of the approach would negate this question, arguing that the only legitimate and necessary outcome of learning is the process itself – it is this that pupils will take with them through life. More realistic responses might note, however, the necessity of qualifications in differentiating ability and effort, thus giving criteria through which employers and agents of higher education can select the most able and appropriate candidate. Such an observation involves compromises to the degree of openness that a process-led programme can have, since fairness would dictate that learners know the criteria on which they are being assessed. Doing so, however, also begins to introduce fixed end points – outcomes of learning – and this, again, sullies the extent to which such curricula can claim to be process driven.

There is also a tension in this regard as to the nature of the content with which individuals engage; this is vague in the original work of Stenhouse. There is an implication, for instance, that such content is necessary – that the kind of broad and balanced curriculum favoured through the liberal tradition should be provided – but that it should never be treated with unquestioning reverence. Such an approach is all very well when it is expressed in idealized terms, but in practice it is very difficult to realize. At one extreme, treating a topic such as electricity as 'intelligent but not necessarily correct' seems tokenistic; it is difficult to imagine a context in which the learner will find such theories to be incorrect. At the other extreme, difficult debates are introduced as to the extent to which unpalatable political stances – neo-Nazism, for instance – should be treated as anything other than patently incorrect.

Stop, Think, Do

Consider the extent to which each of these ideologies has been influential in the educational system that you have experienced. How might your experience have been different if the balance of influences had been different?

Conclusions

This opening section has explored several distinct philosophical paradigms governing what a curriculum should aim to achieve and, by extension, what shape it should take. Each sets out with a very different emphasis – on the syllabus, the skills and competencies desired in learners or the particular processes and experiences to which they should be entitled. Caught up in these differing fundamental emphases are a range of other priorities; thus, theoretical debates implicate a range of other issues. Reviewing the discussion so far, then, a number of key tensions might be identified:

- Should the curriculum appeal to learners' particular needs and talents, or should it aim to extend their experience in a broader way?
- To what extent should the curriculum constrain what happens in schools; on one hand ensuring an equal quality of experience but on the other curtailing teacher judgements and the ability to be responsive?
- What should be the relationship between 'content' and 'the learner' (i.e. what is the preferred pedagogy implied by the curriculum)? What should it encourage: the assimilation of ideas and capacities or critical engagement and reflection?

Viewing the distinctions between theoretical paradigms in this way – and exposing the debates that exist within them – serves as a useful lens through which to 'denaturalize' the curriculum as it currently exists, to see it, not as something obvious and commonsensical, but as something ideologically contested. The next chapter takes this idea forward into reality in examining how these kinds of debates have emerged and interacted throughout history.

The curriculum in a historical context

The contrasting philosophical perspectives which surround curriculum design therefore provide one useful tool through which to unpick how it manifests in contemporary education systems. An alternative, equally enlightening approach is to situate the curriculum against a historical backdrop. In doing so, it is possible to explore the genealogy of key aspects of the curriculum as it currently stands and to expose how many of the taken-for-granted ideas which now seem commonsensical are, in reality, a product of socio-historical invention.

Prehistory: The invention of knowledge domains

As suggested at the opening of this chapter, its aim is to expose two distinct layers of social construction of curriculum. Thus, in this historical exploration, part of the focus is with the actual design of the national programmes of learning found in educational institutions and the role of the theoretical and ideological commitments of curriculum designers in shaping them. We begin here, though, with a deeper concern: the curriculum is itself constructed in reference to a broader system of knowledge, which society divides into particular categories and levels of validity. A manifestation of this can be found in one of the most easily taken-for-granted aspects of the curriculum as it currently stands: the notion that knowledge, and thus educational life, can and should be segmented into subjects. Such an idea is most obvious in the liberal approach, which is very much subject oriented; but even in the instrumental and critical traditions, there is a fundamental assumption that different forms of understanding belong in different conceptual boxes. There are, of course, logical reasons why one might assert that different forms of knowledge are distinct from one another (there is, for instance, an important qualitative difference between understanding in art and science). These divisions have, however, evolved over time; thus, the relevance of distinctions between forms of knowledge is as much a product of historical forces as of logic. It is, therefore, the process of the subdivision of understanding across time with which our exploration starts.

The division of knowledge arises directly from the ways in which humans encounter and experience the world (and thus organize their communities around it). One of the most basic, fundamental ways of doing this can be found in simple tribal societies: the common distinction between religious and mystical understandings and everyday knowledge – between the sacred and the profane (Durkheim, 2008). Viewed from different perspectives, such a division can stand for a range of representations and subdivisions of knowledge. For the communities themselves, they are rooted in notions of the knowable and the unknowable, in those things governed by the direct rules established through experience and those seemingly beyond perception. Alternatively, the division between sacred and profane can be read to be an expression of known and unknown; viewed in this way, one can begin to see some of the ways in which the seemingly concrete boundaries between forms of knowledge might, in reality, be fluid and shifting. So viewed, as communities begin to understand their worlds in more complex ways – that, for instance, weather is governed by season which in turn is caused by orbit – the body of sacred knowledge diminishes and that of profane grows (in effect, what has been called the 'god of the gaps' phenomenon in scientific knowledge).

A similar binary division, distinguishing physics and metaphysics, was expressed by the ancient Greek philosophers in subdividing knowledge. Physics (literally, the physical world) was that which could be derived from direct observation. Metaphysics described forms of knowledge beyond direct observation. While this certainly included matters of a religious and mystical nature, the distinction encompassed more than the division between sacred and profane. Metaphysical philosophy encompassed a whole range of understandings arrived at through reason rather than observation –ethics, politics, law and aesthetics (the nature of beauty). Physics, by contrast, spawned a range of alternative understandings drawn from watching patterns in the behaviour of the natural world. Thus, mathematics, biology, astronomy and medicine all became central concerns of thinkers concerned with physics. It is interesting to note, given the distance that science now places between itself and philosophy, that until well into the seventeenth and eighteenth centuries, scientific enquiry was referred to as 'natural philosophy'.

Of course, religious leaders and philosophers constituted only a tiny subset of society, and the forms of knowledge associated with them were therefore representative of only one fragment of the whole. In addition, a whole range of vocational knowledge forms existed and developed within society – trades passed along through apprenticeship and inheritance. Thus, the basic organization of early societies – and of their experience of engaging with the world – established a set of enduring dichotomies: between the academic and vocational and the spiritual and the corporeal, between that which is known through proof and that which is known through reason. These divisions, in turn, have shaped the structure of knowledge, of education and of the curriculum.

The emergence of formal education

The formalization of knowledge structures into curriculum conventions began with the emergence of formal education in Britain. Thus, the Middle Ages saw the development of two types of institutions of study, distinguished primarily by their curricular focus. One form was the guild school – a centre for vocational study, organized and funded by conglomerates and alliances of local artisans. The other type, primarily religious in tone and directly controlled by the church, existed both to train clergy and to educate the laity in basic religious doctrine (the term 'grammar school', in the UK context, derives from the intensive study of Latin grammar, in which language religious documents were written). In many ways, these divisions between forms of education reflect existing assumptions about how knowledge should be subdivided; notions of sacred and profane, academic and vocational, echo within them.

This era also saw the establishment of universities in Britain; first Oxford, and then, following a disagreement between the people and students of the city, Cambridge. Following established curricular convention, the focus of these institutions was primarily religious, though they quickly acquired a remit beyond the narrow study of scripture. In developing an interest in the study of 'God's work' more generally, they acquired a more outward-looking nature. This was consolidated during the Renaissance, which saw the rediscovery of classical Greek and Roman texts and with them the philosophies of physics and metaphysics. Thus, the universities underwent a transition from religious to academic institutions. Physics became natural philosophy, which gradually splintered into the various facets of science; metaphysics begat politics, ethics and aesthetics, which in turn lay the foundations for literary study and art appreciation. These subjects then underwent combination and recombination into architecture, sociology and other such synthetic domains.

The industrial revolution

Formal education in its earliest days was an elite exercise, enjoyed only by the privileged few. The academic curriculum therefore reflected elite forms of knowledge, valued as much for their association with privilege as for their intrinsic worth. Education as it occurred for the general populace was a more informal affair, and the kinds of practical and vocational learning they required did not seem to necessitate formal schooling. This was, however, to shift with the industrial revolution – a pattern of technological innovation that transformed the economy and created conditions which would necessitate a more encompassing education system. In order to maintain competitiveness, the economy needed a more literate and numerate workforce; this, in turn, necessitated a degree of schooling.

The curriculum within these new elementary schools was, by necessity, something more than vocational training; employers needed workers with a foundation of transferable skills and aptitudes. This is, however, not to say that the introduction of universal primary education was motivated by the kind of liberal focus which surrounded existing academic study. Indeed, such a possibility did not enter into the political debate of the time, which was primarily driven by instrumental concerns (the needs of the economy). It was generally agreed that anything other than rudimentary education for the working classes would be cruel, even dangerous, as it would give them ideas 'above their station'. The consequent curriculum in early primary education, while not explicitly vocational, retained a fundamentally instrumental philosophy. Thus, it aimed to produce workers whose literacy and numeracy skills corresponded to the economy's and employers' needs, and it had values and virtues which would make workers good and efficient. Where other outside content was covered, it was included with the explicit aim of teaching pupils about Britain's (dominant) place in the world and of their place within this. The curriculum could thus be seen to be oriented towards maintaining (and legitimizing) order and stability.

This point in the genealogy of the British curriculum, firmly situating state education (and by extension, the curriculum) in the service of the economy and the workplace, is more significant than it initially seems. In its definition its role was fundamentally and narrowly instrumental – a priority which has shaped the later development of schooling and the curriculum in insidious and overwhelming ways. Having justified the initial creation of state-funded education in reference to economic need, policymakers found it difficult to break from the model and shift to less instrumental forms. This economic priority has influenced many reforms to education, and where the curriculum has drifted away from serving employers, it has fuelled notable backlashes.

This period established a very particular form of instrumental academic state curriculum, but it also saw a parallel development in more directly vocational programmes of learning. In 1878, a conglomerate of 16 trade associations, together with the Corporation of London, formed the City and Guilds of London Institute for the Advancement of Technical Education (CGLI). This group set out to develop a national system of 'technical education', with an associated set of standards and a coherent countrywide qualification system. It established a college in London, which was later incorporated into Imperial College, but its most lasting legacy is found in what is now known simply as City and Guilds, a vocational qualification system offering some 500 awards across 28 industries.

The economic shifts of the industrial revolution therefore formed the impetus behind the establishment of state-funded universal education – and thus access to learning for the masses. The backwash effect of this process was, however, that curriculum development (both in vocational and academic terms) was oriented to the needs of employers and the workplace.

The introduction of state secondary education

Alongside the emerging state provision of education existed a much more firmly established private sector, educating fee-paying pupils through to secondary level. Separate from government funding and thus from the necessity to meet economic needs, these schools, modelled as a scaled-down version of a university such as Oxford or Cambridge, aimed to form a curriculum which was rounded and balanced, with an emphasis on the immersion of learners in the classics as the basis of knowledge. Viewed through the theoretical lens established at the beginning of this chapter, these schools provided learners with a liberal curriculum, while the state primaries were more instrumental in approach. The nature of the hidden curriculum – the values and expectations transmitted by the school to learners – also differed; where the latter aim to produce obedient and hard-working citizens, the private sector emphasized values of competition and individual achievement and thus set out to produce individuals who would become the future leaders in government and business.

The early twentieth century saw the beginnings of a state secondary system in parallel to the private sector's and expanding on existing primary provision. While it retained the instrumental qualities of state elementary curricula, these new secondaries also looked to the existing private sector and thus incorporated a subject-based approach. This was enshrined in law with the 1904 Education Act, which mandated the kinds of things pupils should study in secondary school. It stipulated English language and literature, geography and history, a foreign language, mathematics and science, physical education and housewifery and personal and moral education.

At this point, provision of free secondary education was still sparse; it was not until 1944 that a nationwide system was established. This took the form of the tripartite system, so called because it consisted of three types of school – the secondary modern, technical and grammar schools – to which pupils were assigned on the basis of their performance in an aptitude test called the eleven-plus. The creation of these three types of school formalized and reinforced existing and evolving notions of the divisions between curricular forms. Thus, secondary modern schools became an extension of the academic-instrumental curriculum already present in elementaries – focused on a broad non-vocational education but aimed at developing particular transferable skills. The secondary technical took the baton from the conventions championed earlier by the City and Guilds movement towards quality vocational and industry-specific training. The grammar schools, in contrast, taking as their model the liberal-academic curriculum found in universities and private schools, thus exposed their pupils to high levels of theoretical content – such as calculus in mathematics – and to the canon of classics, from Latin literature through to works of Shakespeare.

Interestingly, this era also saw the integration of religious education as a compulsory aspect of the curriculum regardless of the form of school. This move, however, was motivated more by strategic and political factors than academic or economic ones. Prior to this point, church-run primary schools were excluded from governmental control. The 1944 era, however, saw them become 'voluntary aided' schools – part of the state sector, where they currently remain. Facilitating this shift was an agreement between the government and the church that, in return for control of these schools, religious instruction and an act of collective worship would become compulsory elements of the curriculum.

Curricular divisions were in turn reinforced by an associated emergent system of national qualifications. The existing City and Guilds qualification suite, for instance, validated competence in the vocational learning which occurred in secondary technical schools, while the newly created general certificate of education (GCE) accredited the learner's engagement with the individual academic subjects of the grammar schools. In secondary modern schools learners generally emerged only with a high school certificate, issued by the school itself and indicating that basic education was complete. This, in turn, related to the instrumental nature of the engagement with learning, which was oriented to the development of 'life skills' rather than specific academic understandings.

Progressivism

By the 1950s a fully formed state-funded education system had formed in Britain and with it an established set of conventions about curriculum. The late 1950s and early 1960s, however, saw increasing discontent with both of these, fuelling a progressive turn in education. This backlash against the perceived elitism of the established system led to experimentation in both practice and in curricular provision. On one hand, then, this was a pedagogical revolution, which involved a fundamental shift from teacher- and subject-centred approaches to more student-centred teaching and learning. Such a transition inevitably impacted the nature of the curriculum as applied within schools and classrooms; it provoked a shift to more child-initiated approaches, which emphasized discovery and the development of student interests, and eroded 'the subject' as a central organizing device of the school.

The 1950s and 1960s also saw shifts in the structure of educational provision with the abolition of the eleven-plus and the tripartite system and the rise of the comprehensive school, which set out to educate all children in their locality, regardless of background and abilities. In removing the different types of school, this shift blurred the clear distinctions between vocational, liberal-academic and instrumental-academic curricula. Thus, as a result of their more diverse intake, schools necessarily began to offer a more mixed curriculum of traditional academic subjects, vocational pathways and emerging new domains of study such as sociology and psychology. Crucial to this curricular offering – in an attempt to deal with the limited opportunity created for some children by the tripartite system – was an emphasis on student choice and thus on flexibility for students to pursue their own emerging talents and interests (rather than those identified by a test at the end of primary school). This anti-elitist sentiment also underpinned shifts to the qualification system with the introduction of the certificate of secondary education, a national subject-based examination aimed at those not able to take the existing GCE. With this shift all curriculum pathways received some form of external validation.

The 1960s also saw a significant expansion in higher education with the introduction of polytechnic universities. With this vast growth in the number of places available in post-compulsory education came a consequent reorientation of school curricula in order to prepare students for them. The polytechnics' focus on work-relevant rather than purely academic study is also notable in this curricular discussion. Their creation established the precedent that vocational study could be equivalent in terms of level and qualification to its academic counterpart while at the same time introducing the notion of instrumentalism as a philosophic priority in university-based curriculum design.

The Thatcher government

The next major shifts to the curriculum of the British educational system, some of the most radical in its history, came during the 1980s. There are two key themes in these developments: the first was a backlash against the progressive, student-centred focus which had emerged during the 1960s and 1970s. Political commentators were accusing the movement of having lost touch with the needs of the economy and thus with its purpose. What followed was a wave of 'new vocationalism' – a reassertion of the need for education to have direct relevance to the workplace – and a range of revisions to educational provision and curriculum intended to meet these ends. These included the introduction of compulsory work experience in schools and a reassertion of vocational pathways, including the creation of national vocational qualifications covering plumbing, hairdressing and many other trades. These qualifications reforms were extended in 1992 with the introduction of the general national vocational qualification (GNVQ) and broader industry-oriented qualifications covering subjects such as health and social care rather than specific jobs. This period of vocational reform also saw polytechnics become full-fledged universities in an attempt to erode the 'binary divide' between job-oriented and academic study in higher education.

The intent of the new vocationalism was to reinvigorate employment-related learning and thus ensure that education better met the needs of the economy by reasserting the instrumental model of curriculum. Thus, the reforms aimed to improve the status and coherence of vocational pathways from early secondary through to university-level study. The extent to which the reforms were successful is debatable; they certainly improved the identity of vocational study, though such courses have suffered a persistent perceived inferiority to academic routes, an inequality with which subsequent governments have continued to struggle. The problems of differential status are amplified by systematic social biases among those taking different courses, with the potential of an 'educated' middle class, a 'trained' working class and a recreation of the distinct curricula of the tripartite system.

The second, arguably more important, reform of this era was the creation of the national curriculum. Where new vocationalism could be seen as a reassertion of older priorities of curricular purpose, this strand of reform represented something entirely new and groundbreaking. Where prior governments had legislated around the curriculum in broad ways (in terms, for instance, of the subjects to be covered), this saw the creation of a state-mandated programme of study which not only gave general guidance on the structure of the curriculum but also dictated specific content to be covered. This form of direct and detailed control had been actively resisted by prior governments for fear of accusations of indoctrination and comparison with the totalitarian educational systems of Nazi Germany and Stalinist Russia. The introduction of the national curriculum in the United Kingdom was, however, established with a rationale of establishing standards, thus improving quality of education, and with the argument that without a standardized curriculum, young people were equally open to indoctrination by left-wing teachers. Some distance between politicians and the curriculum was also maintained with the creation of the Qualifications and Curriculum Authority (QCA), a quasi-autonomous organization which would be responsible for the actual day-to-day design and roll-out of the curriculum.

The national curriculum therefore established a precedent of centralized control. It also, however, had philosophical impact beyond defining content in that it embedded instrumentalism into the very heart of programmes of learning by organizing content around learning objectives. Thus, where the principle of utility (or applicability) had previously shaped curricula in general ways (to broadly meet the needs of the economy, for instance), it was now present in the fine grain of subjects. Thus, each aspect of curriculum was justified in terms of a particular competency and behavioural outcome; these in turn formed performative criteria for schools, which could be held accountable via their students' achievements in the SATs.

New labour

In many ways, the reforms to the curriculum during the 1990s and the first decade after 2000 could be seen to be caught in the momentum of those enacted during the 1980s. The national curriculum was reviewed and revised; its scope and mandate continued to grow, increasingly implicating not just the content of lessons but also the pedagogies and approaches through which the content was to be delivered. In an attempt to improve functional skills, for instance, national literacy and numeracy strategies were introduced in 1998 and 1999, respectively. These initiatives included curricular guidance on content and sequence but also went further in supplying so-called frameworks for teaching, which suggested the methodologies that teachers should deploy within their lessons. This government-directed teaching methodology implicitly contained within curriculum structures – what Robin Alexander (Alexander, 2009) refers to as a 'state theory of learning' – has proved insidious. Thus, even when the statutory status of these strategies was downgraded in 2006, schools and teachers continued to conform to them – a product, perhaps, of the regime of prescription, inspection and accountability which had been established over the two decades which led up to this point.

The divide between academic and vocational curricula also retained a central importance under New Labour. The GNVQ was rebranded, for instance, as the AVCE and then the vocational A level in an attempt to diminish the differential status between it and academic routes. A report was commissioned to investigate the 14–19 curriculum. Its conclusions (cf. Tomlinson, 2004) advised that the distinction between academic and vocational pathways be eliminated completely and that the curriculum and qualifications be subsumed by an international baccalaureate-style 'diploma'. In this, all learners would engage with a range of individual units comprising a mixture of academic and work-related study. The advice was rejected, in large part because the abolition of A levels was too radical and politically sensitive to be carried forward. Echoes of the report's sentiments were, however, later to be found in the creation of diplomas – focused on broad fields from 'society, health and development' and 'engineering' through to more directly industry-focused areas such as 'hospitality') – to sit alongside more traditional academic and vocational pathways. These qualifications combined academic and vocational aspects, though their status, in themselves and compared to other routes, is yet to be seen.

The later part of New Labour's period of administration saw growing discontent with the form that had been taken by the national curriculum and with the project of centrally controlled micromanagement of the curriculum. The resultant one-size-fits-all structure of the curriculum was seen as ineffective at meeting the needs of diverse sets of learners; thus, a more student-centred discourse of curriculum (echoing that of the progressivism of the 1960s) began to re-emerge. Two major reports, one independent (Alexander, 2009) and one government commissioned (Rose, 2009), advised major overhauls to the primary curriculum and a move away from prescription and a narrow emphasis on functional skills. Thus, each emphasized a need to shift away from overemphasis on literacy and numeracy (and in general on instrumentalism) to provide a broad and balanced curriculum. A second common emphasis was on the need for a more 'creative' curriculum, one which broke away from traditional subject boundaries and allowed for teaching which was more thematic and more focused on the children's own development. Thus, the Cambridge Review – arguably the more radical of the two publications – suggested a shift from subjects to eight 'domains': arts and creativity, citizenship and ethics, faith and belief, language, oracy and literacy, mathematics, physical and emotional health, place and time and science and technology.

Future directions

This book is published at a time of political flux, following a general election which brought to power a coalition of political parties. Predicting future directions in education and in the curriculum within this climate is difficult; the contradictory messages that have so far emerged make prediction all the more challenging. On one hand, the new government is committed to the notion of relaxing central control of the curriculum, giving teachers and schools more power in its design. To this end, they have encouraged the establishment of 'free schools' and academies, which enjoy a greater degree of autonomy than local authority–maintained equivalents. At the same time, however, they have pledged a set of 'back to basics' reforms, with an emphasis on reviving traditional subject boundaries and a knowledge of core ideas within them. To this end, they have repealed reforms which had been enacted in response to the Rose review (see discussion above). They have also abolished the QCA, the organization previously tasked with oversight of the curriculum. The implications of this move remain ambiguous. On one hand, it might be read as a delivery on the commitment to relax control over the curriculum. Equally, however, without an autonomous body tasked with its oversight, the curriculum is in the direct control of the ministry of education and, thus, potentially under the control of politicians to a degree unprecedented in history.

Stop, Think, Do

Examine a range of recent newspaper articles on the curriculum. To what extent do current directions in policy reflect historical trends? To what extent do they represent new ideas?

Conclusions

While the curriculum as it currently stands may appear to be a neutral and commonsensical structure, it is in reality a site of ideological, philosophical and political contest. Its purposes, its aims and whom they should serve, the degree to which it should be standardized and the extent to which central government should have involvement in this process: all of these generate myriad competing perspectives and debates. In turn they connect to broader issues underpinning educational policy and practice: the tensions between teacher- and student-centred learning, the problems of inequity and differential achievement and the role of education in ideological control, to name but a few. As this chapter has shown, it is possible to begin to denaturalize the curriculum and to expose these tensions and debates by situating it in both a philosophical and a historical context. In doing so, we are able to better appreciate the degree to which different logics compete within the design of curriculum – syllabus, outcome and process – and the ways in which curriculum structures, as they currently stand, have been shaped by broader political and economic pressures. Having reached this point, in the chapters that follow, we explore notions of power and resistance surrounding this process before exploring one further influential factor shaping curriculum: technology.

Key questions

- What do we mean by 'curriculum'?
- Which philosophical and ideological models underpin debates on curriculum design?
- What are the key distinctions between liberal, instrumental and critical approaches to curriculum?
- How do each of these stances approach the process of curriculum design?
- What are the key overlaps and distinctions in different ideological and philosophical approaches to curriculum? What do these reveal about the tensions underpinning curriculum design?
- How has the curriculum currently in place in England and Wales evolved historically? What does this reveal about the social and political influences on the shape of curriculum?

Further reading

Alexander, R. (ed.) (2009). *Children, Their World, Their Education: Final Report and Recommendations of the Cambridge Primary Review*. London: Routledge.

Freire, P. (2001). *Pedagogy of Freedom: Ethics, Democracy and Civic Courage*. New York: Rowman and Littlefield.

Hirst, P., and R. Peters (1970). *The Logic of Education*. London: Routledge and Kegan Paul.

Joseph, G. G. (2000). *The Crest of the Peacock: Non-European Roots of Mathematics*. London: Penguin.

Rose, J. (2009). *Independent Review of the Primary Curriculum: Final Report*. Department of Schools, Children and Families. London: Crown.

Knowledge, Power and Ideology

5

Chapter Outline

This chapter will examine the development of a centrally controlled curriculum and teacher training. It will outline the development from organizational control, length of days, exams and the like towards focused control over content and will examine the pressure upon government from various influential groups, such as the humanists, and the importance of the Black Papers (1969 onwards). This outline will lead to a discussion of James Callaghan's 1977 Ruskin speech and the controversy over the William Tyndale School. The historical background will draw students into a discussion around the concept of hegemonic control (Gramsci, 1935) and the naturalization of the status quo. The chapter will also examine the concept of knowledge as a series of agreed truths (or otherwise) and furthermore examine the modernist and postmodernist approaches to the development and transmission of knowledge.

Introduction

Parents have never been able to access so much information about either the schools that their children attend or those in which they are considering enrolling them. From league tables to OfSTED reports, the supposed quality of each school is laid bare and open to public scrutiny. Recent plans to expand this information to include teachers' qualification levels and pay bands, together with the numbers of children eligible for free school meals and those with special educational needs (DfE, 2010), will increase the range of information available to parents. The question remains as to how useful much of this information actually is and, perhaps more crucially, the purpose behind it.

This level of information is not possible unless parents have some common standards with which to compare schools and their performance. It is worth noting that the publication of school results in the form of league tables from 1992 is highly problematic, and as Tomlinson (2005) states, such results demonstrate the social-class composition rather than the educational performance of an area. The issues of social class determining educational outcomes is long established and is not the purpose of this chapter (see Murphy et al., 2008, for a fuller discussion). However, the policy reforms which the league tables are part of illustrate the increasing level of central and local government control over schools, the curriculum and the training of teachers. As Apple puts it, 'Formal schooling is by and large organised and controlled by the government. This means that by its very nature the entire schooling process – how it is paid for, what goals it seeks to attain and how those goals will be measured, who has power over it, what textbooks are approved, who does well in schools and who does not, who has the right to ask and answer these questions, and so on – is by definition political' (Apple, 2003, 1).

A historical context – towards increased control

Political and societal control over education is not a new concept, and the role of education in developing individuals who will take up a place within a wider functioning society has long concerned educational theorists. Plato began his own discussion of education with the words 'These are the kind of people our guardians must be. In what manner, then, will we rear and educate them?' (cited in Kelly, 2004, 161). Direct and recognized governmental influence over education is a relatively recent phenomenon, but it is worth noting that indirect control over issues such as school starting and leaving ages, the types of exams taken, the length of the school day and school inspections are long established, and all have influenced the curriculum, although in a less focused way than the current system under which our schools operate. In fact there was widespread political and social opposition to governments becoming too involved in the content of the curriculum, and the idea of a national curriculum when first discussed in the 1930s was rejected as 'smacking of totalitarianism', as it was largely countries led by dictatorships which felt a need to directly control the education of the next generation. Hitler felt the need to re-write school textbooks and created schools which promoted the Nazi ideal and through direct influence over subject content attempted to ensure that the next generation was fully indoctrinated into the idea of a German master race. The curriculum content of geography was redesigned to discuss issues about the unfairness of land taken from Germany under the Treaty of Versailles following the First World War. Similar attempts to control the thoughts of the young were established in the old USSR. While we should clearly draw no comparison between Hitler's attempts to control education and our current national curriculum, it is clear why opposition to any state control over education during that time period would be so strong in England.

The Butler Education Act of 1944 established the 11-plus examination, where children were tested at the end of primary school; their results determined the type of school they subsequently attended. The brightest and most academically able went to grammar schools, where they focused on preparation for university. The most technically gifted supposedly went to technical schools, although few were built, and the remaining students went to secondary modern schools to undertake a more general curriculum. Concern was increasingly expressed that social class determined the most likely destination for children, with grammar schools largely and almost exclusively populated by children from the higher socio-economic groups (Martin, 2004).

To address this problem, an attempt was made in the 1960s under Harold Wilson's Labour Government to create a new type of school for children from all socio-economic groups in an effort to alleviate the increasing educational disparity in terms of success. In addition, as the early stages of a knowledge-based economy required a well-educated workforce to meet its needs, the economic impact of educational failure started to be felt. This newly created type of school was called a comprehensive (many readers of this book may well have attended such a school). This new approach met with fierce opposition throughout the 1960s and 1970s, as politicians from the political right and their supporters in the media systematically attacked the rise of comprehensive education and the expansion of higher education, The right-wing politicians and the media claimed that attempting to provide a more suitable education for all of society was in effect 'dumbing down' and lowering standards all round. They further stated that it was an attempt at social engineering that would destroy academic standards (Tomlinson, 2005).

In conjunction with the changing political nature of education, significant changes in teaching practice were gaining currency within the classrooms. The concept of child-centred or progressive education was considered to be rife within the schools of the period. This was arguably fuelled by the Plowden Report of 1967, which advocated a more progressive and child-centred approach to education to combat the current system, which was said to have contributed to educational inequality largely based on social economic status. Progressive education was certainly not a new idea, and its genesis can arguably be found in Rousseau's seminal work *Émile*, written some 350 years ago in 1762. Within the text Rousseau's main thesis is that rather than adults determining what children should know, it is essential to focus upon what a child is capable of learning and upon issues which are rooted within the child's own experience. In a standard lesson a teacher provides knowledge to the student which the student reflects back in terms of an appropriate response. This can be likened to a mirror, which provides a reflection but no internal understanding of the concept; likewise, the student does not internalize or fully understood the issue, as it is not presented with reference to his or her own experiences (Darling and Nordenbo, 2006). This concept of rooting ideas to a child's experience is echoed in the work of Piaget (see Chapter 1). This progressive approach to education naturally does not lend itself to agreed content or a subscribed pedagogical approach. Later in the chapter we will examine the critique that a progressive approach provides to the concept of agreed and important knowledge, but at this stage it is important to understand that this teaching approach was heavily criticized by a range of parties, including politicians, commentators, the media and business. As Tomlinson (2005) points out, the evidence suggests that, in the majority of schools of the period, education was anything but progressive and that, instead, teaching methods tended in the main to follow a didactic approach common to many people's educational experience. However, the perception of the left-leaning radical and progressive teacher was a powerful one, which the media and other interested groups targeted to challenge the purpose of the education system. That system came under attack from two main ideological approaches. The first, the humanists, advocated a curriculum based primarily upon traditional culture and classic texts and languages, including the canon of English literature, together with a focus on the three Rs; the second approach is that of the industrial trainers, such as the Confederation of British Industry, who bemoaned the fact that education was not providing individuals with the necessary skills and knowledge for the workplace, although as Kelly (2006) points out those skills have yet to be adequately explained or articulated. It is of course not immediately obvious how these two quite distinct approaches could both be incorporated into an education system, but the basic message of a system not fit for purpose was one that clearly resonates with politicians, parents and wider society.

In 1969 a series of Black Papers was published, led by Brian Cox and other eminent thinkers and commentators of the time, perhaps most notably Kingsley Amis. These papers were severely critical of educational policy in terms of comprehensive schools and, in particular, the liberal and progressive teaching methods within schools, including mixed-ability classes. They stated that this approach had led to a decline in academic standards, an increase in bad behaviour within schools and pupils' views being unduly influenced by left-wing teachers. These highly influential papers, with their advocacy of selection for schools based on academic merit, of a return to traditional teaching methods and subject matter and of a higher priority for basic skills, merely present an approach to education which could be equally criticized and challenged, but at the time they caught and reflected the mood of the nation.

Perhaps the event which most cemented the public, rather than media and academic, opposition to the notion that schools were overrun with left-wing radical teachers adopting a progressive teaching approach and denying children access to knowledge occurred at a school in Islington, the William Tyndale School. In 1974 the school, which had declared itself a commune, was run in a fully progressive manner, challenging what they saw as an unfair educational system which blighted the lives of many working-class children and ensured that those from the highest socio-economic groups would always achieve more, an educational system that maintained and perpetuated an unequal and divisive society. The issues within the school came to public attention when a teacher, Annie Walker, stated that the methods employed denied children basic knowledge and the chance for academic progress. In taking her criticisms to the parents of the school children, she brought the school to the attentions of the national media and forced the Inner London Education Authority (ILEA) to take action. The subsequent public enquiry was a media circus, and the apparent failings of the school were extrapolated to place the whole concept of progressive education and the school system on trial. While the William Tyndale School did have a range of issues, its 'failings' had the much wider implication of moving educational policy closer to interventionist strategies in schools (Davis, 2002).

In 1976 James Callaghan, the then Labour prime minister, delivered a speech at Ruskin College Oxford, where he controversially stated that schools and the teaching profession were failing to meet the needs of the economy and, therefore, society:

I am concerned on my journeys to find complaints from industry that new recruits from the schools sometimes do not have the basic tools to do the job that is required.

He further stated that the purpose of education was not being met:

The goals of our education, from nursery school through to adult education, are clear enough. They are to equip children to the best of their ability for a lively, constructive, place in society, and also to fit them to do a job of work.

And that parents and society did not have a clear idea of what was happening in schools:

It will be an advantage to the teaching profession to have a wide public understanding and support for what they are doing.

In what can be seen as a clear call for a national curriculum, a standard inspection regime and more direct comparison between schools, Callaghan stated,

Let me repeat some of the fields that need study because they cause concern. There are the methods and aims of informal instruction, the strong case for the so-called 'core curriculum' of basic knowledge; next, what is the proper way of monitoring the use of resources in order to maintain a proper national standard of performance; then there is the role of the inspectorate in relation to national standards; and there is the need to improve relations between industry and education. (Callaghan, 1976; cited in *Guardian*, 2001).

Prior to Callaghan's speech high unemployment among teachers, due to falling school rolls, provided an opportunity for the DfES, as it was then, to raise entry standards for all teachers and thus, for the first time, create an all-graduate profession. By also giving the department the power to control numbers of trainee teachers in universities, the standards gave the government increased powers, through the allocation of those numbers, to heavily influence the type of training that teachers received within the universities. As Kelly (2004, 174) states, '[I]t is no great step . . . from that kind of control to control over the nature and content of the curriculum of these courses'.

All of the above events culminated in the 1988 Educational Reform Act, under the then Conservative Government. This act, for the first time, introduced a centrally determined national curriculum in the schools, which provided a list of core subjects – English, mathematics and science – and introduced national testing at ages 7, 11, 14 and 16, known as Standardised Assessment Tests (SATS). The road to this act was a long and controversial one, and the cementing of the national curriculum in the Dearing Review of 1993 ensured that no longer would schools and teachers be able to determine the content of their lessons nor in any way respond appropriately to the culture of the children they teach. The Dearing Review also stated that no changes could be made in the content for a 5-year period, a quite bizarre announcement in a rapidly changing world. The national curriculum also introduced local management of schools (LMS). This enabled schools, if they wished, to opt out completely of local government control and reduced the powers of those local authorities, such as ILEA, to influence schools and schooling. While the attempt to centrally control content but allow schools to manage themselves financially and broadly take control over the hiring of staff may seem counter-intuitive, it actually ensured that central government removed a tier of control that had existed between them and the schools. In essence, it further strengthened centralized control (Ward, 2004). In 1992 this control took a new direction with the development of the Office for Standards in Education (OfSTED), which inspected all state schools every 4 years. This is often seen as a rather blunt instrument which fails to recognize the local pressure that schools can operate under and instead assesses according to a list of prescribed standards. The subsequent publishing of those reports together with league tables outlining each school's performance in the SATS, regardless of the social intake of students, at least initially, led to what many see as a concerted attack upon the profession of teaching. The impact of published results in the form of league tables should not be underestimated. Schools which have an intake from areas of social deprivation invariably find themselves towards the foot of those tables. When parents are looking to choose a school, those with the capacity to move and enter the catchment areas of more successful schools will do so. This relocation can result in certain schools becoming sink schools, and thus social mobility remains difficult if not impossible to achieve (Jones and Mitchell, 2009).

While initially the national curriculum focused only upon subject content and left how to teach up to the individual teachers and schools, a report by Alexander, Rose and Woodhead in 1992 advocated whole-class teaching and streaming of pupils by ability, among other suggestions. Therefore, since 1930 and a suggestion that prescribing content could be seen as totalitarianism, in 60 years not only was a national content imposed upon schools, but also an increasing influence on the ways teachers taught and how they were trained was implemented. By supporting this with a public and national inspection regime, schools and teachers felt under increasing pressure to operate according to a set of prescriptions.

Stop, Think, Do

Ask older people for details about their school days. Consider some of these areas as prompts:

- the structure of the day;
- the age they started and finished;
- the subjects they studied;
- the exams they took;
- the role of parents;
- how boys and girls were treated and the differences within education;
- the types of jobs they were considering;
- school trips;
- teaching and learning styles;
- types of resources they had;
- the role of peers.

Do you feel that their experience was very different from your own, and if so, in what ways?

Did their experience suggest an education system that was too progressive and radical?

Teacher training – new developments

As previously mentioned, teaching became an all-graduate profession in the early 1970s, a development initially due to an oversupply of teachers, many of whom were unable to find positions in schools. The control over numbers of teachers gave central government increasing control over what training teachers received within universities. If standards were not seen to be met, numbers could be reallocated to other institutions, thus ensuring a more standardized approach to the training. In initial conception, the theoretical basis involved trainee teachers studying issues such as the philosophy, sociology and psychology of education, together with opportunities for practice within school settings. This approach came increasingly under attack not only from central government but, interestingly, also from the trainees themselves, who tended to prefer the practical elements to the theoretical perspectives. This led to the formulation of the Council for the Accreditation of Teacher Education (CATE) in the 1980s, which changed and developed into the Teacher Training Agency (TTA) in the 1990s and later the Training and Development Agency (TDA). Overall the changes introduced longer placements within school, at the expense of educational theory and an agreed set of professional standards which teachers had to achieve in order to gain qualified teacher status (QTS). Ward (2008, 18) claims that this lack of theoretical perspectives does not provide students with the critical analysis necessary for any profession. Therefore, instead of viewing education and teaching as challengeable concepts, depending on circumstances both in and out of the school, the current system is more focused on competencies and a set of key skills. Newer initiatives, such as Teach First, provide even less opportunity for theorizing and reflecting and can result in teachers being given their first class to teach after 6 weeks of intensive training, albeit with ongoing support. The coalition government, the ConDems, elected in 2010 are widely expected to further reduce the role of universities in the training of teachers with a suggestion that the training of teachers take place within the schools. This is not a new idea; similar attempts failed in the late 1980s, but the idea that teaching is an uncontested enterprise that can be reduced to a set of skills and is classed as 'training' rather than 'education' has been gaining currency over the last 30 to 40 years and is likely to reach its ultimate destination in the ConDems' educational White Paper. What impact this will have upon the professional nature of teachers and their ability to respond to local needs and the individual needs of children remains to be seen. We all remember our best teachers (see Bates and Lewis, 2009), and while the reasons we remember them differ, one common theme is that of understanding. They understood our needs and adapted to provide the best experience for us. Without true opportunities for reflection and a knowledge of theoretical perspectives, not to take wholesale but to consider their value and role within education, are we in danger of losing the best teachers to a more focused and competency-based approach?

Agreed knowledge

We began this chapter with a quote by Michael Apple, who states that control over all aspects of the school sector of the education system is in the hands of central government. We can see from the discussion above that in our system here in England, this includes the content of the curriculum, preferred teaching methods, an inspection regime which publishes its results and control over the training and development of teachers. We may now start to question the impact of this control and what its purpose may be and what impact it has.

The testing regime and increasingly standardized approaches to education in schools suggest both an agreed approach to teaching and learning and that success of any child in school is mainly to do with the quality of the teaching and the provision that they encounter. Value-added scores on league tables, which assess the child's progress over the period in the school, go some way to acknowledging that social factors such as parental qualifications, ethnic group and socio-economic status have an impact upon the levels of achievement within schools. The reasons why are not for this chapter to examine; more information can be found in Mufti 2008, but it does give a clear indication that a one-size-fits-all approach is not currently meeting the needs of large sections of our society.

Callaghan in his Ruskin speech suggested that education, at the time, was not meeting the needs of society or the economy. He laid the blame on progressive educational methods, which ironically were established in an attempt to alleviate inequalities based on some of those factors outlined above. We can see from many newspaper and radio debates that business and industry are still not satisfied with the current provision; so we can ask what has been achieved by this standardized approach?

The national curriculum sets out the most important content and standards that children should achieve at various age groups. What is though the most important content? Whose perspective is being promoted in the teaching of, for example, history? Do we have a structural approach to content in that it can be seen as unchanging and not fully subject to enquiry?

An ideological challenge?

To present knowledge as unchanging, as the Dearing Review suggested in 1993, suggests a system of knowledge which is agreed and eternal. Marx believed that ideological positions of unfairness and educational inequality are implicitly supported by the imposition of agreed knowledge and that by agreeing knowledge we further agree the societal systems which are in place. In essence, when we agree knowledge, we further agree a set of norms and values within the education system and within wider society. Marx felt that there was nothing natural about modern society, that it was merely a construct and one that could have been constructed in a variety of alternative ways. Marx suggested that the dominant ideology, which would be supported by a nationally agreed school system, has three main functions: first to naturalize; that is, to present any system, such as UK society, as naturally occurring rather than conceived and created. This, of course, would render any fundamental questioning of it as superfluous. Secondly, that it historicizes, presenting the status quo as a natural progression rooted and supported in history. The third and final aspect is that it eternalizes; that is that the system is eternal and any attempt to alter it would be seen as regressive, taking us backwards in development rather than forwards to a better and fairer society.

In a response to this approach, many neo-Marxists, including Freire, Giroux and Apple, have advocated a critical pedagogical approach in schools and education. This approach would be to enlighten groups about the inequalities of society and allow them to critique, fully understand and ultimately challenge the dominant system (Mufti, 2008).

Other approaches in terms of challenging agreed knowledge, values and norms can be found in the concept of postmodernism. This complex and changeable perspective is not always easy to define and pin down. Effectively, it relates to many of the issues that Marx highlighted above in that we should question the validity of knowledge, thought processes and what may appear to have been agreed positions. This approach can lead to difficult discussions around concepts of what is right and what is wrong. What types of moral codes should we employ, and how would society function in that case? (Peters and Wain, 2006).

All of the above approaches could arguably be contained in the demonized 'apparent' system of the 1960s and 1970s, that of the progressive movement in schools. As previously discussed, this system was widely criticized. However, its basic premise, that education should be child-centred, relevant and reflect the culture of the classrooms and schools, is hard to argue against. In fact many of the ideas of the progressive movement have found themselves a home within the modern classroom and are perhaps no more or less prevalent across the whole sector than they were during the William Tyndale crisis. As Pestalozzi (1807) stated,

The teacher must enter wholly into the child's point of view, identifying himself completely with the purpose in hand and march in company with the child from truth to truth, discovery to discovery.

This approach, as you can see, is easy to critique because we are used to a more didactic teaching approach where the teacher has the knowledge and decides how, and in what ways, it should be best presented. It is more difficult to assess learning, due to the fact that a more personal approach is implemented, one in which neither a standard curriculum nor a standardized assessment strategy would fit neatly. Perhaps the curriculum and its approaches are being shaped more by assessment than by the true needs of children.

Free schools

If there is one thing we have learnt from any historical study of educational practice it is that history has a habit of repeating itself. It is clear that the national curriculum has not significantly changed the levels of educational inequality within the system. You are still far less likely to succeed if you are from a lower socio-economic group or from particular ethnic groups. The current government, building on the academy idea of New Labour, have responded to this by promoting the development of free schools. These schools (DfE, 2010) can be set up by parents, charities, businesses and, interestingly, groups of teachers. How they will operate and for what purpose those groups will set up a free school remains to be seen. However, the new government suggest that they are aimed at challenging disadvantage, particularly in deprived areas. Ironically of course, this approach to schooling, which seeks to challenge levels of inequality, could be a description of the William Tyndale School. The government is not allowing total freedom, however; the schools will still be accountable to inspections, and their progress and achievement will be tested. Currently free schools will be able to opt out of the national curriculum, and Michael Gove, the education secretary, has suggested that teachers will have more autonomy and the opportunities to make more decisions about the best approaches to take in terms of pedagogy and content. What the impact of this will be remains to be seen, but it proves once again how changeable and open for debate educational practice is and therefore asks serious questions about the approach to education and teacher training we have endured for the last 25 years.

Conclusion

It is clear that education is a central part of our society and that we all – whether we study, teach, have children at school or are simply part of society – have a vested interest in the sector. Educational success benefits us all, and educational failure damages us all. The best approach to education is not clear, and the history contained within this chapter shows how we are still struggling to agree upon a system. The rise of free schools, arguably again, demonstrates the difficulty of trying to agree upon a national set of standards and approaches across a diverse and complex society. The de-professionalism of teachers and the removal of theoretical and reflective perspectives from their training have left them less equipped to meet the challenges of that society. While complete freedom for schools and teachers may be unwelcome, it is no more a problematic position than imposed standards and a negative inspection regime.

Key questions

- Is there such a thing as agreed knowledge?
- Do you feel that a critical pedagogy in schools would be an improvement to the current system?
- What might a system based on critical pedagogy look like, and what impact might it have?
- Should the educational system focus on the economic needs of society?
- What might be lacking in such an approach?
- What types of free schools are being planned? For what purpose?

Further reading

Apple, M. (2003). *The State and Politics of Knowledge*. New York: Routledge.

Bates, J., and S. Lewis (2009). *The Study of Education : An Introduction*. Continuum: London.

Hatcher, R. (2001). 'Getting down to business: Schooling in the globalised economy'. *Education and Social Justice*, 3 (2):45–9.

Kelly, A. V. (2004). *The Curriculum: Theory and Practice*, 5th edn. London: Sage Publications.

Murphy, L., E. Mufti and D. Kassem (2008). *Education Studies: An Introduction*. New York: McGraw-Hill.

6 Knowledge as Resistance

In the previous chapter we discussed the development of state control over schools, the curriculum and, increasingly, pedagogy. The 2010 White Paper 'The Importance of Teaching' has mixed messages about this approach. On the one hand, it discusses reducing the level of control, but further rhetoric suggests that in many areas this control will be strengthened. This chapter is not concerned with the mechanics of state control but with the impact that it has upon various groups within society.

The level of achievement among young adults taking their GCSE exams has risen year on year, and the numbers gaining five passes at A to C levels have increased from 57 per cent in 2003 to 67 per cent in 2010 (DSCF, 2010). While this is a commendable increase and it is important to not detract from those individuals' achievements, it is worth noting that not all groups in society are as likely to achieve this level of success.

Those groups are varied and complex but include issues such as the ethnicity, sex and socio-economic status of the pupils. All of these factors contribute to the chances of an individual gaining five A-to-C GCSE passes.

The chapters in this book outline the historical development of knowledge together with the learning styles that teachers are expected to adhere to in terms of delivery. In many ways this suggests a somewhat unproblematic response to learning and teaching whereby individuals respond to stimulus and input in terms of their learning approaches. However, as we will discuss, the various learning approaches are not the only factor we need to take into account when examining achievement. We also need to consider the culture of the individuals, sometimes as part of a group, and the issues influencing them outside of the school environment, including parental support, role models and the perceived role in their community, for education to create change.

Social class and educational achievement

In 'The Case for Change' (2010), the ConDem government cite Feinstein (2008) and state that 13.9 per cent of the variance in performance of pupils in England can be explained by social class. While they suggest that these figures are a challenge, it is worth referring back to Marx's ideas about a natural, historical and eternal state of affairs (see the previous chapter), of which 'who does well in education?' could be seen as a primary example.

When discussing social class in education, we tend to use the short-hand measure of eligibility for free school meals as an indicator. While this is far from unproblematic and can often be based on income and, for example, a change in family circumstances rather than an interpretation which will focus upon attitudes and long-term life chances, it still remains a way to gain an overall picture of the impact of social class. In 2010, 54 per cent of children eligible for free school meals achieved the expected level (4) in English and maths in the Key Stage 2 SATs, compared with 76 per cent of children overall. Therefore, at the age of 11 there is a clear indication that children from lower socio-economic groups are doing significantly less well than their better-off peers. This led Michael Gove to make a rather blunt comment, 'Rich thick kids do better than clever poor ones.' Although this comment rightly received criticism, it does highlight that at every stage of the educational experience social class matters. This chapter is not concerned so much with the reasons behind these difference, as this has been discussed at length in other studies and books (Mufti, 2008; Hatcher 2004); instead it will focus on the intervention attempted and planned and whether this focuses on the right issues. The debate here will rest upon whether it is the responsibility of the child (and perhaps the family) to fit into the education system or whether the system itself excludes and disadvantages certain groups. Furthermore, we will examine the ways in which groups resist the educational system and how that can impact upon levels of success.

Deficit model of education

Many of the initiatives proposed or already in place to combat this level of inequality tend to focus on ensuring that individuals can 'fit into' the system more effectively. Therefore, the new pupil premium (DfE, 2011) will be given to schools in order that they can spend additional income on those pupils deemed to be at a disadvantage. Schools will have the responsibility for how they spend this money, but it is unclear as to what would be deemed acceptable when they are held to account. It is likely that success will be determined in terms of academic results.

> Whilst schools will be free to spend the Pupil Premium as they see fit, they will be held accountable for how they have used the additional funding to support deprived pupils. New measures will be included in the performance tables that will capture the achievement of those deprived pupils covered by the Pupil Premium. (DfE, 2011)

While it may be hoped that this extra money goes some way to reducing inequality, it is worth pointing out that myriad initiatives and changes to the education system within this country have not alleviated the levels of educational differences attributable to social class in any meaningful way.

Too often we focus on the idea of a 'deficit model'; that is, that the individual pupils or the social groups that they belong to are the problem rather than the system. As Valencia (1997) suggested, the most powerful group that sets the agenda, ways to achieve success, acceptable modes of behaviour and methods of engagement, and it is the responsibility of the pupil to conform or falter. This idea of course links to the argument in other chapters of this volume, that we are too reliant on a one-school-fits-all policy, which maintains and promotes failure of certain social groups.

If we take the view that it is the responsibility of the pupil to fit into a system, we are placing the emphasis upon the children and their families to change. We need to question whether this is viable, achievable and ultimately desirable. While initiatives such as Sure Start could be said to operate in this manner, we need to question whether this is the right approach; if tweaks to the current system were what was needed, then would we not have begun to eradicate the problems outlined above far earlier? It can be said that the lack of achievement among certain groups has led to the adoption of a counterculture which clashes with the dominant culture and ethos of the system (see Chapter 8). While this could be seen as related to an individual's lack of progress within the system, it could also be seen as a more politically aware response, whereby individuals are aware of what is needed to succeed but choose not to as a direct challenge to what they see as an unfair and unjust system. In discussions around the achievement of boys and students from minority ethnic groups, the lack of appropriate role models is often presented as a major cause for concern. Male educational role models in the school, home and community can be conspicuously absent for boys from lower socio-economic groups and in particular black Caribbean boys. This has a dual effect in that there are few who understand the particular needs of these children, who then adopt a counterculture unsuitable to successful academic performance as evidenced by the work of Sewell (1997) and Willis (1977). It should be noted that this counterculture is a response to a system which is not designed to meet their needs, as they see little or no evidence of past achievement among those they would respect. Much of this is due to increased levels of single, predominantly female, parents coupled with a lack of male teachers within the primary school. There is also the wider issue of a narrow curriculum which lacks role models. As Abbot (2005, 109) states, 'Black boys need men in the classroom. They simply do not see reading or educational attainment as masculine or cool'. Abbot further links this issue to that of white working-class boys. While there are male role models, they rarely come from backgrounds similar to those students most at risk in the system.

Parental involvement and the home environment

The impact parents can have on the educational progress of a child has been known for some time. In 1967 the Plowden Report built on a range of research which demonstrated the correlation between parental interest and the educational progress of the child. Nor is the role that parents play in their child's education lost on national government. Through the Sure Start initiative for families with children under 4 and a number of information sources, including *Parents' Magazine* and the DfES website, the government seeks to ensure that as many parents as possible have access to resources that can facilitate them in supporting their children's education. Recent proposals to increase parents' authority have also been included in various educational policies, with the latest policy (2010) giving them the right to open up their own schools (this subject is discussed in Chapter 8). The level of academic achievement of a child's parents has proven to be a good indicator of academic success for the child. The suggestion is that these parents are more likely to see the value of education and aid their child's development. This of course might suggest that those parents who do not perform well have a less-developed interest in their child's education. While it is true that increased involvement correlates with higher levels of success, the issue is more complex than that. The idea that parents from lower socio-economic groups do not have an interest in their child's education is an over-simplification; in fact, evidence from Topping and Wolfendale (1985) is just one of many examples which show that parents of all class groups have an interest in the education of their child. The main difference lies in the ideologies they have around education as a positive or negative force, ideologies which have been shaped by their own experiences. Furthermore, issues of cultural capital and an awareness and knowledge of the system ensure that parents who have previously succeeded in the system are able to navigate their way through its intricacies much more effectively.

Stop, Think, Do

What role do parents play in education?
Consider how your parents helped you? Were they involved? In what ways?

Bad behaviour and poor results or resistance and rejection?

Perhaps it is time to rethink the educational approach we take in England if we truly wish to engage as many groups and individuals within it as possible.

In their review of the literature of social class and educational inequality, Perry and Francis (2010) make a distinction between the types of interventions which have sought to address this issue and highlight the areas which appear to have been neglected. The initiatives that have been tried or are still in place have primarily fitted firmly within the deficit model:

- a meritocratic approach that targets individual high-achieving, working-class young people;
- a focus on raising aspirations of individuals and their families;
- a focus on academic routes and on prestigious universities and career paths;
- a focus on attainment, rather than engagement with education.

In contrast, Perry and Francis (2010, 16) state that too few, if any, have taken a more system-changing view, such as:

- focusing on educational engagement and ownership by working-class young people, as a precursor to achievement;
- addressing working-class young people as a group, irrespective of ability; emphasizing collectivist rather than individualistic approaches;
- paying attention to vocational routes and careers in addition to academic routes;
- focusing on and valuing the existing knowledge forms of working-class young people.

In addition, many of the new initiatives outlined by the ConDem government can be seen to have the capacity to increase inequalities and conflict between teachers and pupils.

First, the idea of the English baccalaureate will redefine levels of success as achievement within a range of narrow subjects, namely, English, maths, science, history or geography and a language. Leaving aside the arguments as to whether these are even the most suitable subjects, where is technology for example? The idea that we place further restrictions of what is success is likely to negatively impact those from lower social groups. Second, concerning ideas around discipline and the use of mobile phones, Michael Gove (2011) recently outlined plans which would allow teachers not only to confiscate phones but also to delete content which they deemed inappropriate. This imposition of cultural norms and values suggests an agreed definition of what would be deemed acceptable content is surely debatable and this approach would ensure an imposition of a dominant culture thus further ensuring that within the school rules. While there may be content which we as a society would deem unacceptable in all circumstances, this would clearly leave many grey areas and the potential for huge conflict between schools, teachers, parents and pupils. It is unclear whether what is seen as unacceptable content would be debated in classes such as RE or PHSE.

These approaches, both from the current and the last government, still maintain what is fast appearing to become an illusion: that by focusing on raising an individual's aspirations, we can alleviate social-class difference within education. Perhaps what we need to consider is to what purpose that would be?

Current figures suggest that there are 976,000 young people unemployed within England (*Guardian*, 2011). Disproportionately, these youngsters come from lower socio-economic groups. Furthermore, pupils from the lowest socio-economic groups are less likely to gain entrance to university and significantly less likely to gain access to pre-1992 Russell Group universities, which the government are keen to promote as containing the best future teachers, for example ('The Case for Change', 2010). In addition to the changing nature of the economy, jobs being outsourced, a rise in 'knowledge-based jobs' and subsequent decline in manufacturing, heavy industry and low- and semi-skilled jobs have meant that the future for those who do not achieve in education is worrying at best. Furthermore, we have to look at this issue in a wider context and ask whether merely reducing the gap in terms of educational inequality and raising the levels of academic success for all groups would result in more equal entrance to higher education and jobs. We know, for example, that many students with high qualifications are still not accepted to Russell Group institutions, and as many of them come from state schools we must ask whether we are focusing too much on trying to raise standards without challenging the barriers that society will place in front of individuals from lower socio-economic groups.

Media interest in 'chavs' and gang culture have arguably further reinforced the point that attitudes, accents, ambition, access to extracurricular activities, social manners and interests can all combine to make it less likely for certain individuals to achieve high levels of success no matter how well they perform in school. This leads us to an argument that it is not just the education system that disadvantages groups; society and its structures also play a major role in strengthening that level of inequality. If this is the case, is educational non-conformity a way of protesting against an unequal and unjust system?

If we take this argument forward, low- and high-level behavioural problems and lack of conformity and interest in education can be seen not as issues that require intervention aimed at the individual but instead as legitimate challenges to an unequal society of which schools are one part. Effectively, why attempt to do well in school when the opportunities an education may offer to others are likely, or appear likely, to be closed to you?

Stop, Think, Do

Do people have equal opportunities in school and in the wider society?
Is a person, regardless of background, as likely to achieve as anyone else?

Bowles and Gintis stated that the messages we gain from schools correspond closely with the world of work we later encounter. This is part of what Hatcher (2001) would call the 'capitalist agenda for schools', in that the purpose of education is to create subservient workers within a capitalist economy. These workers will have the necessary knowledge to be productive, but, far more importantly, they will consider the working environment as natural and unchangeable and one they should work within rather than seek to alter. For Bowles and Gintis education corresponded with the world of work in a number of key ways. First, they stated in their study that grades related more to subservient personality traits than to ability. In addition through school, pupils learn the hierarchal nature of the educational environment in the way that the teacher is in charge and above her lies the deputy and the head teacher. Bowles and Gintis claim that an uncritical acceptance of these power relations will smooth the educational progress of the pupils much as it would within a work environment. The idea of external rewards through the exam system and their role in gaining higher status employment also link education to the work place in terms of exam results being equal to wages. In much the same way that employment may be unsatisfying and unrewarding with only the prospect of a wage making it worthwhile, the learning process is equally unrewarding, with the result being many children fail to enjoy school. However, the carrot remains in terms of external rewards: in one case wages, in the other exam results.

While the importance of the work of Bowles and Gintis should not be underestimated, there are a number of criticisms of their work. Some of it focuses upon their reasoning and research methodologies, but, perhaps more tellingly, criticism is also levelled at the way in which they present children as uncritical and unquestioning adopters of the messages within the hidden curriculum. Bearing in mind that theorists such as Bowles and Gintis form part of what we class as the conflict theory of education, there is little evidence of conflict within their work. This has led to the likes of Apple (1998) and Giroux (2001) to criticize the work as being somewhat misleading. It is worth noting though that Bowles and Gintis (2001) reject such claims.

A lack of conflict and awareness of what is occurring in education is not a criticism that can be levelled at Paul Willis, who, in his seminal text *Learning to Labour: How Working Class Kids Get Working Class Jobs* (1977) discovered strong evidence of a rejection of school and the formulation of a counterculture among working-class pupils. Willis followed a group of 12 boys for their last 18 months of school and into their first jobs. The 'lads', as Willis coined them, had clearly rejected the messages sent to them via the hidden and official curriculum. They had little respect for teachers and more subservient pupils and realized instinctively that the rewards of good performance in school were not applicable to them as they had no prospect of succeeding within the system. This was not, as Willis states, a politically aware decision, and, in fact, the racism and sexism of the boys was contrary to such an awareness; instead, the awareness was developed from observing those around them from similar backgrounds within their homes and the community. Their peers in this case obtained jobs primarily in semi-skilled and unskilled labour towards which schools had little to offer. In fact though, once Willis followed the boys into their first jobs, he discovered that what was classed as a counterculture within schools was the dominant culture within those workplaces. Therefore, the rejection of the school culture was born out of the school culture having little relevance to their own. They also realized that academic qualifications were unlikely to be achieved within such a system, which, Willis argued, was developed to exclude too many of their class from achieving.

In many ways Willis's ideas link to Francis and Perry's (2010) suggestions for strategies to alleviate individual differences by focusing on changes to the system and, rather than concentrate on individuals, concentrate on the needs of the group – in this case, those from lower socio-economic backgrounds. This attempt to take the focus away from the individual is a subtle but important distinction, as it is far easier for educators to place the blame on the attitudes or abilities of a pupil than suggest that the system is at least complicit in ensuring their failure. If we are forced to examine the issues faced by the group, we are led into more uncomfortable but, hopefully, ultimately rewarding discussions around institutional and societal inequalities. As Willis himself put it,

> Insofar as knowledge is always biased and shot through with class meaning the working class student must overcome his inbuilt disadvantage of possessing the wrong class culture and the wrong educational decoders to start with. A few can make it. The class can never follow. It is through a good number trying, however, that the class structure is legitimated. (128)

Here Willis is stating that by focusing on the individual, we ignore the wider implications of large numbers of a particular group failing to achieve.

If we are then to challenge more structural inequalities, in what ways would education need to change?

The idea of identity is strong in Willis's work, and more contemporary examinations of this issue by people such as Evans (2007) and Mount (2010) suggest that identity can often be found in countercultures rather than those which would be more expected by society and the education system.

The work of Paulo Freire (1998) has resonance here in that, through his work in Brazil, he criticized an education system which devalued the levels of knowledge, history and engagement of those from lower socioeconomic groups. Freire suggested that the relationship between the teacher and pupil was unequal and that it disadvantaged those whose values and ethos did not mesh with those in the positions of power:

> A careful analysis of the teacher-student relationship at any level, inside or outside the school, reveals its fundamentally narrative character. This relationship involves a narrating Subject (the teacher) and patient, listening objects (the students). The contents, whether values or empirical dimensions of reality, tend in the process of being narrated to become lifeless and petrified. . . . The teacher talks about reality as if it were motionless, static, compartmentalized, and predictable. Or else he expounds on a topic completely alien to the existential experience of the students. His task is to 'fill' the students with the contents of his narration. (Freire, 1998, 54)

Freire was heavily critical of the social construct of that knowledge, and from that we can infer that knowledge is not only straightforward, as in terms of kings and queens of England, but also complex and designed to ensure that certain issues are not challenged or broached. This could implicitly include issues around who gains access to the better jobs and more powerful positions in society (see previous chapter). The example of kings and queens is a timely one given that rhetoric from the ConDem government and Michael Gove has focused on pupils learning facts such as these, whereas a more appropriate challenge to the inequalities may come from addressing the underlying principles of class and status which negatively impact upon our society. Freire suggested an approach which is echoed by Francis and Perry (2010); namely, to value and focus on the existing knowledge of pupils, therefore potentially making education more meaningful to a wider range of pupils. Freire suggested that teachers should add curriculum developers, express humility and promote the fact that knowledge is constructed and not an absolute. His approach suggested a system of dialogue where knowledge is debated, critiqued and ultimately created through a partnership between students and teacher. This, he felt, would be more likely to lead to what he termed praxis, that is, action with reflection. This would result in a challenge to unequal systems, as students would possess the knowledge and understanding of both unequal systems and ways in which to challenge this. Freire felt that you needed both action and reflection as one without the other would lead to activism, which is action without thinking, or verbalism, which is thinking without action. Perhaps we can see activism taking place both within schools, manifesting itself as countercultures and poor behaviour, and in wider society as anti-social behaviour, youth crime, disengagement, countercultures and protests from anti-capitalist groups and, more recently, students.

Freire's ideas can be found in Giroux's (2001) suggestion of a critical pedagogy which has at its aim a challenge to the unequal nature of education. Giroux suggests that both what we teach and the way that we teach it create and maintain inequalities based upon cultural, social and economic attributes. It is worth noting here that Giroux suggests the system is designed to operate in this manner and is not merely an unintentional consequence. Giroux felt that this manifested itself in a variety of ways. First, the superior status of high to popular culture suggests that the culture that many pupils enjoy out of school has no place and is derided within it. Secondly, through the removal of history of those from lower social classes and minority groups and thirdly through racial and culturally specific language which seeks to stigmatize others and create barriers which certain groups find difficult to overcome. Giroux however, does offer solutions to the current system. Much of it based on local schools meeting local needs. For example, Giroux suggests that schools should become an integral part of their community and should reflect the values and ethos of that community rather than one which has been imposed centrally. He suggests that teachers and community members should be seen as co-owners of knowledge and the educational process and should collectively determine what is taught. Giroux also believed that schools should promote public values and reject the ideology presented by big business, competition and individualism. Instead schools should encourage pupils to be socially critical and promote empathy and collective responsibility. He stated that teachers should be aware of the ideological framework of the knowledge they present and of the fact that this knowledge is determined by time, culture and those in positions of power. This, of course, would require teachers to be given far greater autonomy in the way in which they work and would no doubt lead to a rejection of the removal of universities for teacher training and a subsequent lack of opportunity for reflection.

Education for all?

We can see clearly from the above discussions that social factors influence children's levels of achievement, but we need to begin to consider why this might be.

One of the main criticisms of the ConDem government is the idea that the Cabinet, in particular, is drawn from a too-narrow social group. Many of them were privately educated, and at the time of writing 18 of them were millionaires. While this in itself does not preclude them from making decisions which impact upon the education of all children, it brings the issue of the nature of education and educational policy further into the limelight. Effectively, if certain groups of children are not achieving as highly as other groups, is this the fault of inequalities within the system or with their own levels of engagement and perhaps ability.

Conclusion

There is no doubt that not all pupils achieve the same levels of success within our school system. Too often and for too long, this discrepancy has been largely based upon an individual's background in terms of ethnicity, gender and social class. These issues are not separate entities and we all categorized into those groupings in so much as we are all of a gender, ethnicity and social class grouping. At times those groupings combine and can lead to the detriment of the life chances of certain individuals. This chapter has concerned itself with these issues. Should we continue to place the emphasis of change upon the pupil or consider ways in which the system can reflect the culture and background of all pupils more effectively? In essence, how much of educational success can be attributed to what occurs within schools and how much is related to external factors such as those outlined in this chapter. The ideas in this chapter suggest that the system is unequal and that those who suffer within it are fully aware of this and in a variety of ways seek to challenge it. At present that challenge impacts negatively upon them in terms of lack of opportunities, but educational failure at this level impacts all of society. The challenge we face is not one merely of improving education but of challenging inequalities in the wider society, which means that for certain groups, success in education carries less weight than it does for others. This issue links strongly to Chapter 8, 'School Ethos and the Role of Teachers'.

Key questions

- What role did your parents play in your education?
- Have you been part of or witnessed a counterculture in school? Why might it exist?
- Do you agree with Bowles and Gintis that school is a preparation for work?
- Do we still have a class-based society? Examine the background of some who hold positions of power. Did ability or a biased system get them where they are?

Further reading

Abbot, D. (2005). 'Teachers Are Failing Black Boys', in B. Richardson (ed.), *Tell It Like It Is: How Our Schools Fail Black Children*. London: Bookmarks.

Bowles, S., and H. Gintis (2001). 'Schooling in Capitalist America: Revisited'. e\papers\JEP-paper\sociology of education.tex.

Evans, G. (2006). *Educational Failure and White Working Class Children in Britain*. Hampshire: Palgrave MacMillan.

Hatcher, R. (2004). 'Social Class and School', in D. Matheson (ed.), *An Introduction to the Study of Education*, 3rd edn. London: RoutledgeFalmer.

Mount, F. (2010). '*Mind the Gap*': *The New Class Divide in Britain*. Croyden: Bookmarque.

Sewell, T. (1997). *Black Masculinities and Schooling*. Stoke-on-Trent: Trentham Books.

Willis, P. (1977). *Learning to Labour*. Farnborough: Saxon House.

7 Knowledge and Technology

Technology is a buzzword in the current British educational system. With the proliferation of new tools – the interactive whiteboard, the virtual learning environment, and on the like – have come claims of a revolution in pedagogy and a radical transformation in educational provision, experiences and outcomes. The impacts of these technologies are clearly important (though they also deserve critical treatment), but in this chapter the reader is invited to consider the educational context of technology in a deeper and broader way. To maintain the focus of this section of the book, the intimate relationship that technology holds with society's knowledge structure and systems – and thus with the basis of the curriculum – is considered first, then its consequent impact on educational systems and practices. The intent in taking this approach is not to deny the potentially revolutionary impact of technology on educational practice since in many respects quite the opposite is true. In considering these impacts at a more fundamental level, the chapter will highlight that their nature is potentially *more* revolutionary than current pedagogical applications imagine. In equal measure the chapter also aims to suggest that utopian visions of technology as an educational 'golden bullet' are misplaced and that a critical lens is necessary to mitigate an array of potentially negative effects.

Discussions of technology seem, impulsively, to reach first for the radical innovations in computing and networking which have occurred in the past half-century. Such an impulse is, however, myopic; it fails to appreciate a deep and profound history, a reciprocal relationship in which advances in knowledge and understanding have facilitated the development of new technologies while these technologies, in themselves, have radically transformed the production, organization and distribution of knowledge.

We begin here, then, by exploring a selective treatment of this history, organized around three key technological revolutions. Such an approach is revealing, first, in the ways it demonstrates how technologies now considered mundane had impacts which were as profound and revolutionary as, if not more so than, more contemporary ones. Secondly, it begins to reveal a sense of the ways in which some of the tensions surrounding knowledge and technology are situated in a much broader context and time frame.

Stop, Think, Do

List all of the technologies with which you engage as part of your educational experience; include 'new' ones, like the computer, but also more mundane artefacts such as the pen and pencil. Reflect on some of the ways in which these technologies shape and influence your experience of education and learning.

The first information revolution

The short-sighted treatment of knowledge and technology often involves a conflation of *technology* and *high technology* and frames the discussion in terms of relatively recent innovations. In reality, however, *technology* extends to any means by which humans adapt their environment in order to meet their needs. In this respect *technology* can refer to anything from the wheel to the aeroplane, the flint to the modern production line, the pen to the computer. In equal measure, *technology* refers to the know-how and expertise used to adapt that environment using these tools; indeed, in the German origins of the phrase, the notions of 'technique' and 'technology' are much more closely associated. Thus, technology can also be conceptual; it can comprise the metaphors and ideas used to render sense into our environments. Viewed in this way, perhaps the most important technological revolution in the history of the human species is the invention of language, without which the division of the external world into categories, and the communication of these categories, would be impossible.

Language made it possible to formalize knowledge within small communities, reifying the belief and value systems of small societies in the form of oral histories and folk tales. Early religious myths, for instance, provided a mechanism to bind tribal communities through a commitment to a shared world view and to transmit these basic means of dividing and understanding the reality within which they exist to new generations (Levi-Strauss, 2001; Malinowski, 1978). The units of knowledge encoded within these stories were, of course, dependent on tellers for their existence, and the role of storyteller in oral cultures was (and is) one which confers a high status, precisely because stories embody and reproduce a society's world view and knowledge system. This dependence, however, also means that knowledge systems tend towards instability and gradual distortion over time. Viewed historically, they are also relatively immobile; unable to spread beyond the immediate context of the small-scale community. All of this was to change, however, with a technological innovation which signified the first – and arguably most important – information revolution of human history: the invention of writing.

Nascent precursors to writing, the encoding of meaning in a graphic form, have a long history. Cave paintings, for instance, can be found that are some 25,000 to 30,000 years old (in Nambia and France, respectively). These systems were largely iconic; representing meaning in images which corresponded to their physicality in reality, they depicted (and recorded) everyday activities and concerns of the people who produced them. By the seventh century BCE, these systems had, however, evolved in their sophistication and in the complexity of information that they could convey. In the case of one of the best-known early-writing forms, Egyptian hieroglyphs, these systems retained an iconic quality in that they had the surface appearance of real-world objects. They also possessed, however, a much deeper symbolic nature, with icons indicative of sounds in spoken language (hence, the first notions of alphabet) and of concepts beyond the initial surface representation. They also represented the advent of syntax, with the meaning associated with words modified by their organization and collocation. Elsewhere, writing was more directly symbolic and consisted of series of marks and lines to denote letters – as found in writing systems such as cuneiform (in ancient Sumer). As an efficient, quick method of encoding spoken language, this system gained dominance in the Western world, evolving through the ancient Greeks and Romans into the alphabet as it currently stands.

Since it is an activity and skill now taken for granted, it is easy to understate the significance of writing in transforming human knowledge. With its invention, ideas could be recorded in concrete ways and, thus, become stable and portable to an unprecedented degree. Distortions in telling became less pronounced, and thus a community's knowledge system could be sustained across time – Europe's Renaissance, for instance, was founded on a rediscovery of ancient Greek and Roman thinking – and could be shared far beyond its immediate context. This in turn facilitated not only the spread of ideas but also a cross-pollination of understandings across cultures and geographical boundaries. This new-found mobility and stability enabled, for the first time, development to occur at exponential rates through a march of progress, with scholars studying and building on ideas developed and documented by their predecessors. As a result, great schools of understanding began to emerge among the ancient civilizations, canons of understanding in, for example, biology, ethics, astronomy and mathematics throughout China, India, Greece and the Arab world.

The written word, in this respect, also facilitated a transnationalization (a globalization, even) of ideas, as individuals physically transported written accounts of knowledge. A pinnacle of this process in the ancient world was the library at Alexandria – a vast complex, built in the third century BCE, housing academic and literary texts imported from around the ancient world. Under mandate of the Egyptian ruling classes, scholars were sent to import texts and (according to legend) borrow and copy books from every ship that landed at the local seaport. Having become one of the largest repositories of information and understanding in human history, the library in turn attracted thinkers from around the world to use its resources. As a result, the centre became a building not only for the storage of knowledge but also for its generation – a precursor to the research traditions in modern universities.

We should recognize, of course, that reading and writing at this point – and throughout the Dark and Middle Ages – was an elite exercise, dependent on the expert status of a relatively small number of literate individuals who, in turn, were generally a part of the ruling classes of society, of the church or of the royal courts (in some ways, an elite position which echoed that of the storyteller in preliterate society). Thus, from this early period in history, the production and distribution of knowledge and access to it became intimately associated with power in overwhelming and insidious ways. From this point onwards, the 'written account' began to assume a level of truth above anything else; those with the capacity to produce this account therefore gained control over what was considered to be legitimate by society. A reciprocal relationship evolved: those in power, by merit of their literacy, were able to have their agendas encoded as society's official knowledge structure, and this in turn served to legitimize their interests. Access to this information was, of course, also mediated by this expert status, and the illiterate masses remained dependent on local religious officials to read (carefully selected) texts to them. Thus, literacy brought with it power – at the local community level, too, as it allowed local leaders to maintain their status and privilege. Even where, by outside chance, members of the laity were able to read, their access to information was still limited – in part because texts were usually written in Latin, rather than locally spoken languages, and because the hand-copied nature of books made them exorbitantly expensive.

The second information revolution

In considering knowledge and technology, then, the invention of the written word stands out as the most significant innovation in history – and remains so to this day. It is only through writing that it became possible to develop and share a stable canon of knowledge and, with it, the basis of a curriculum. Since this point, though, other technological innovations have shifted the nature of writing, with an impact on knowledge which is similarly radical and revolutionary. In our potted history of the most significant of these innovations, the next was to occur in

1440 in the workshop of a German goldsmith and inventor named Johannes Gutenberg, who had constructed a contraption which lowered moulded metal blocks, dipped in ink, onto a sheet of paper in reliably steady ways. Gutenberg had, of course, produced the world's first printing press, and the broader economic, social and political ramifications it presented would mean that the world would never be the same again.

The printing press enabled, for the first time, the mass-production of the written word. Where previously a single scribe might produce around 2 pages of text per hour, an operator of a Gutenberg press might produce close to 240. When these hand-operated presses were later replaced by steam- (and then electric-) powered ones, this figure grew exponentially, until, by 1818, presses were capable of producing nearly 2,400 impressions per hour. With this growth, books – which had been a rare and expensive commodity – became much more available, in terms of both quantity and affordability. What was once an artefact to be owned only by a privileged few was now reasonably accessible to society at large. With the growing availability of printed texts, literacy among the masses began to rise, freeing them from a dependence on religious and legal figures for access to knowledge. Perhaps one of the early printed texts most symbolic of this process was Martin Luther's German translation of the Bible – significant because not only was it possible for households to possess their own Bible but also, free from the dependence on Latin (because it was not under the direct influence of the Latin-centric Catholic Church), they could study and understand it for themselves, significantly eroding the need for (and thus the power of) the church. In Britain, the Tyndale Bible (printed in 1525) similarly attempted to bring religious texts to the people; it eventually evolved – by 1611 – into the official King James Bible which stands today.

Where the printing press revolutionized access to knowledge, it also impacted on its production. The development of commercial printing houses diminished the reliance on the scriptoria of monasteries or courts in the publication of books; thus, profitability, rather than papal or national decree, became the key principle governing whether a text could or would be published. This shift is significant in that it led to an explosion in the sources of publication and in the perspectives represented in the 'written account' which forms the basis of society's knowledge system. This is, of course, not to say that the printing press heralded a complete democratization of the production of knowledge – after all, there were still significant social biases in those who found themselves able to make representation to the publishing houses. It did, however, prompt a multiplication in the number of perspectives produced. According to Eisenstein (2005), the printing press therefore had a contradictory impact on the society's knowledge systems. On one hand, it created a uniform point of reference and thus concretized orthodoxies and dogmas – many of the 'taken-for-granteds' of the modernist construction of knowledge. Equally, though, it facilitated the distribution of alternative perspectives working against these conventions and thus encouraged a counter-hegemonic strand.

Beyond these macro shifts in the nature of knowledge, the printing press also heralded a more personal and internal shift – to the methods individuals use to think about and engage with formal knowledge. Marshall McLuhan argued that the printing press brought with it the rise of the 'alphabetic monopoly' – a shift from a cultural mindset reliant on auditory information, image and decoration to one in which the letter ruled supreme. As a result, aesthetics became less important and the centrality of 'lines of argument' became more significant – something that was to fuel an explosion in scientific thought. He also notes that '[p]rint exists by virtue of the static separation of functions and fosters a mentality that gradually resists any but a separative and compartmentalizing or specialist outlook' (McLuhan, 1962, 126). In other words, the rise of the printed word encouraged the formalized sectioning-off of knowledge into discrete and isolated units – things that underpinned the evolution of the notion of curriculum subjects – a process, as we will see later, disrupted by newer online technologies. Later in his work, McLuhan generalized from this principle to argue that any new technology ultimately impacts not just on the availability and production of knowledge but also on how individuals think about the world – and thus on how they organize and interact socially. Famously, he summarized this principle in the dictum 'the medium is the message' (McLuhan, 1964; 1967).

The third information revolution

The ways in which the printing press – as it was steadily improved in efficiency and capacity – impacted on the construction and distribution of and engagement with knowledge are deep and significant. No other single innovation approximates these effects, but the contemporary era heralds the promise of a new technological revolution, one which might even rival the printed word's. The past century has seen the rise of electronics and of digital representation of information – typified by information and communications technology and, most significantly, by the internet. These have the potential to transform society's engagement with knowledge in new and radically different ways.

While the internet typifies this revolution and forms the major focus of this chapter, it is perhaps better considered as something much broader. The electronic (then digital) revolution is underpinned by the gradual growth and popularization of what have now become (through an array of other technologies of mass production) consumer media technologies – beginning with the radio in the early twentieth century and spanning the invention and popularization of television and then the multichannel mass broadcast systems of the current era. In some ways, the impacts of these technologies can be seen as a natural continuation of the trend started by the printing press: that of making more and more information available within the home and thus of democratizing access knowledge. The impacts of these media on the perceptions of geography are particularly noteworthy, bringing far away places into the home and thus apparently shrinking the world so that it resembles a 'global village' – a term coined by McLuhan (1962) to describe the ways in which new electronic media speed up the flow and spread of information across vast distances. These broadcast media also emphasize linearity and genre in knowledge – in the same way that the printing press enshrined them in text – and thus reinscribe the boundaries between subject domains. Contrary to McLuhan's observations on the printing press, however, broadcast media generally diminish the alphabetic monopoly – the reliance of culture on the printed word. Rather, they promote resurgence in the visual and the auditory modes as representations and explorations of knowledge. Note, however, that while these modes of representation have grown in dominance within the popular consciousness, there remains a cultural bias towards the written word in terms of what constitutes the most 'valuable' forms of understanding.

Among these electronic technologies, the computer has emerged as emblematic in having particularly notable and particularly different impacts on society's knowledge systems and the ways in which people engage with them. While these impacts feel relatively recent, in reality 'electronic computing' has a history comparable to the transistor radio, in that the first computing device was invented in the 1930s. Early development was slow, and in 1948 Thomas Watson, chairman of IBM (what was to become a major computer manufacturer) famously declared, 'I think there is a world market for maybe five computers'. The technology did, however, take hold – initially as a technical tool, deployed by researchers in universities, where the computer often occupied entire rooms. Even at this early point in its history, though, the computer had a major impact on knowledge production, facilitating the processing and compilation of huge datasets in a relatively efficient way. The 1970s saw the invention of the microchip, which replaced bulky valve and transistor machines with much smaller and, eventually, much cheaper ones, paving the way to a mini-revolution through the 1980s and 1990s, which saw the rise of the home computer.

Alongside this evolution in hardware was a parallel development in the ways in which computers were able to connect and communicate with one another. The internet as we now know it began in the 1950s as a US military project, one which attempted to decentralize storage of information by distributing it across a widespread network (thus, if one node was compromised, the rest would remain safe). It quickly became a safe and efficient way of coordinating projects across the various US Department of Defense research centres (often based in universities). ARPANET, the first 'inter-network', was born. Through the 1970s and 1980s, this form of network became globalized and was coordinating research efforts across academic departments in many countries through JANET. Already, the technology was revolutionizing knowledge by facilitating an unprecedented level of cooperation and collaboration in human enquiry. It was, though, ultimately a closed system, navigable only by those with specialist understanding of how to access it and with the specialist equipment to do so.

All of this was to change in 1989, when Tim Berners-Lee, a British information technology contractor at the CERN laboratories, published a paper which aimed to standardize and simplify communications across the internet. He suggested a series of protocols which would allow documents to be linked using a special markup language called hyper-text; with these suggestions, the World Wide Web was born. The significance of this move could not be understated; it made searching the internet and navigating the information found there accessible, and it signified that the network could have a mass appeal. In the early 1990s, the first commercial internet-access packages were offered; since then, connection to the global network and the number of pages it contains, the speed of connection – all have grown exponentially. By 2000, there were 300 million internet users, producing around a billion pages. At the time of writing (2010), this number had grown to 1.8 billion users who, together, have written just over a trillion distinct pages.

While the protocols and surface structures of the World Wide Web that were established at the early points in its history remain its foundations, the web's nature has shifted subtly as users have engaged with it over the past 20 years. In its original incarnation, the web was a pre-dominantly 'read only' experience – users posting pages of information for others to access – with little genuine 'interactivity' beyond where it was explicitly mandated, such as in forums and chat sites. There has been a gradual shift, however, culminating with the arrival of 'Web 2.0', in which websites provide the infrastructure to facilitate and host user-generated collaboration on content. Perhaps the most notable example of this trend is Wikipedia, an internet-hosted encyclopaedia, in which articles are written and moderated by everyday users.

The internet constitutes a technological innovation with the potential to revolutionize knowledge production, organization and access – though we should also note that, in these early days and without the benefit of hindsight, its impact is still somewhat unpredictable. At the very basic level, though, one crucial feature is the sheer *amount* of information that it makes available to everyday people, dwarfing that of the printing press. The internet as it currently stands would take 57,000 years to read – or if one were so inclined, 3,805 years to print on a stand-ard desktop printer. Such a figure, substantial in itself, also has potential impact on how individuals engage with knowledge and understanding. It has, for instance, eroded the need for information to be committed to memory, as content is now easily available at the touch of a button. The internet has, according to some theorists, become like a prosthetic brain, an external space where knowledge and understanding are stored for individuals as and when they need it (Dalrymple, 2010; Pickover, 2010). The implication here is that an understanding of facts has declined in importance, while a corresponding ability to process, transform and critically assess information has become more crucial – a matter that, in and of itself, has proven to be a point of contention. On one hand, theorists influenced by a behaviourist stance (see Chapter 1) are dubious about the loss of information retention as a mechanism of learning – a perspective echoed by some political commentators (Gibb, 2010). Elsewhere, theorists with a leaning towards information processing (see the segment on Cognitive Perspectives within Chapter 1) and those emphasizing utilitarian and social learning (see Chapter 2) herald such a shift as positive.

A second key impact of the internet as a repository of knowledge is that it represents information in a non-linear way. Where books and, to an extent, television and other broadcast media tend towards a fixed sequencing of information and a compartmentalizing of content (see discussion of McLuhan above), the internet is, quite literally, organized as a web. As such, it encourages a meandering approach to information – one jumps from content to content on the basis of usefulness and apparent relevance rather than according to strict subject-domain criteria. Thus, it echoes some of the broader postmodern currents in culture, notably the growth of a pick-and-mix, hybridized orientation to truth and understanding.

We are, then, beginning to realize the potentially significant effects that the internet may have on the ways in which individuals access and engage with knowledge. There is also, however, a reciprocal theme to be found in the ways in which it transforms the production of knowledge. The internet represents an unregulated and fundamentally democratic space in which everybody can have a voice – at first (under web 1.0) in publishing one's own website and later (in web 2.0) in contributing knowledge to a broader repository of content. Such an arrangement facilitates an increased level of alternative perspectives – pluralism in knowledge – which again connects directly to the postmodern shift in culture. It also goes some way to decoupling the production of knowledge from profitability (a major influence in the production of print) and thus enables a less market-driven distribution of understandings, ensuring that the perspectives represented are not just those which appeal to a perceived mainstream audience.

Significantly, the internet also provides an unrivalled medium for collaboration; this is perhaps its most fundamentally revolutionary impact in terms of the production of knowledge. Sites such as Wikipedia provide a place in which expertise can be combined and through which the synthesis of competing perspectives can be used to generate new ideas (one only needs to examine the discussion pages which lie behind Wikipedia's front end for evidence of this). This model of collaborative and non-commercial production is inspiring new and unusual working practice; the model of open-source software design (in which many authors contribute to a final piece on the basis of social need rather than profit) is to be found elsewhere, such as in the production of research.

The internet, then, has the potential to revolutionize both access to and production of knowledge in fundamentally democratic ways. It is, however, easy to fall into a trap of viewing the technology through a utopian lens, one which views only its positive potential and omits the very real risks inherent to it. It is, therefore, worth devoting a little time here to critical reflection on the negative impacts of the internet on knowledge. On one hand, the erosion of hierarchies and absolute authorities on the internet – the right for everybody to contribute – also brings perils in terms of trustworthiness, with no inherent mechanism to ensure that content is balanced or even true. It might be argued that, for example, in order to publish a book, an individual must have proven authority within a particular field – an inbuilt reliability filter (of course, this can never be assumed to be wholly true!). On the internet, though, this being absent, web pages can be more liberally filled with personal opinion and hearsay.

In respect to this theme, the open-contribution model of Wikipedia has generated interesting debate. It might be suggested, for instance, that this leaves the source open to misinformation, omission and out-right malicious modification; all of these certainly occur across the site. Equally, though, the site administrators point to its peer-refereed nature, in which articles are subject to public scrutiny and ongoing modification and revision at a level far beyond that possible with a printed text. Through this process, errors are eventually corrected, and extremes of opinion or representations are gradually balanced out through a law of averages. Some studies (e.g. Giles, 2005) have suggested that, as a result of these mechanisms, the error and omission rates of Wikipedia are actually comparable with printed encyclopaedias – though the studies are often based on a limited, random sample of pages, and often point to a poorer written quality in the online sources.

A second problem with the utopian view of the internet's impact on knowledge relates to its assumption that such effects are fundamentally democratic. Such a view is blind to the realities of internet access and the inequalities therein. Statistical evidence disturbs the assumption that internet use is equally distributed; it highlights consistent social biases – a 'digital divide' – with certain groups unable to access the internet and thus disenfranchised from the benefits it promises in terms of both access to and production of knowledge. In Britain, for instance, 10 million people have *never* used the internet (Pollard, 2009); that is the equivalent of 25 per cent of the adult population – the combined population of the United Kingdom's five biggest cities – while only 63 per cent of households have broadband internet connections. These internet-disadvantaged individuals are in turn disproportionately drawn from marginalized sections of society: the elderly, poor, disabled and the like.

Viewed from a global perspective, these inequalities are all the more pronounced. The vast majority of internet users originate in the world's most developed countries. Europe and North America – which together account for 16 per cent of the world's population – contain 38 per cent of its internet users (Internet World Stats, 2010). At the other end of the spectrum, Africa – home to 14 per cent of the world's population – accounts for only 5 per cent of its users. Elsewhere in the world, the distribution seems more equitable; Asia, home to 56 per cent of the global population, accounts for 42 per cent of internet users. Even here, however, there are stark inequalities between richer and poorer sections of the region – in Asia, for instance, access is disproportionately biased towards countries such as South Korea. Even where access to the internet is possible, a further layer of global inequality can be found in the language through which information is expressed. More than 80 per cent of the web is in English – and 90 per cent of all web traffic, including emails, chat and so on – compared to a global population only 20 to 30 per cent of whom are capable of understanding English.

Viewed through this lens, the claim that the internet is a democratic and equal space seems somewhat less compelling, for only the privileged few have access. In turn, and in a reflection of earlier relationships between technology and knowledge, it is these individuals who are able to validate their perspectives on the world and who are able to access broader repositories of understanding. This notwithstanding, the potential – if not yet the reality – of the internet as a mechanism for transforming knowledge remains substantial.

Stop, Think, Do

Consider the ways in which the structures and processes of education have been shaped by the historic technologies which were utilized within it (e.g. the extent to which the textbook has been an influential factor in presenting knowledge). How might newer technologies offer radical challenges to both curriculum and pedagogy?

Education and technology

So far this chapter has shown how society's knowledge system has been intimately intertwined with its technologies, with revolutions in the latter transforming how understandings are constructed, communicated, distributed and engaged with. In turn the education system – as a structure which defines itself in relation to that knowledge system – has been shaped and distorted by that technology. The final segment of this chapter considers this relationship, exploring how the practices and systems of education in the Western world, as it currently stands, have been constructed in relation to dominant technologies and how new digital innovations have the potential to fundamentally alter these structures.

Perhaps the most overwhelmingly influential technology on current educational practices and structures is writing. A graphological bias pervades the current system. This assertion may seem commonsensical and entirely reasonable – the skill of writing is, of course, crucially important to any individual. It is, however, interesting to reflect on the degree to which performance of knowledge (proof that one understands) in the current system is predicated on the ability to produce a linear written account. Thus, examinations and essays dominate the British qualification system, from early SAT tests through GCSEs and A levels and into higher education; indeed, as an individual progresses through these phases, writing's importance becomes ever greater. Even in the early phases of primary education, the importance of writing is notable, with activities centred on exercise book-based work. In emphasizing writing in this way, other modes of expression are assigned a lower status; for instance, the status assigned to expression through talk, dance or art leads to the perception of them as less valuable and legitimate (indeed, learners are often asked to produce a written account in order to justify their non-written products). Arguably, then, this single technology shapes educational practice in overwhelming ways.

Beyond this aspect of education, technology's historical legacy runs even more deeply; the system is formed around structures and processes introduced by the printing press. On one hand, this can be seen quite literally in schools' continued reliance on textbooks. There is, however, a broader resonance in this influence, as the use of the book as a central artefact of education has shaped how the system (and the curriculum) is oriented around knowledge. Printed texts, for instance, both embody and reinscribe hierarchical power and authority structures surrounding knowledge. In suggesting, for instance, inexorable and unquestionable sources of truth, by extension they marginalize those not included within them – whether omitted aspects of the 'official' account of understanding or the informal, 'unofficial', understandings of the learners themselves.

As implied through the discussion of McLuhan (above), the book can also be seen as being responsible for propagating a sense of containment and segmentation in knowledge. It draws, in fixed, linear ways, divisions between different domains of knowledge: the arts and sciences and fact and fiction, for instance, live in entirely separate texts, while different topics within them should be segmented into different chapters. These structures, though taken for granted, are inherent in the ways in which dominant models of curriculum are designed according to subjects and strands. Equally, the dominance of the printed text on education has shaped the pedagogical practices by which individuals are asked to engage with the curriculum. Reading printed text or writing is ultimately a solitary activity; it has produced what Seeley-Brown and Adler (2008) refer to as the Cartesian model of learning. Referencing the philosopher

Descartes and his famous maxim, 'I think therefore I am', they argue that this set of practices, common in contemporary education, focuses on the transfer of substance (formal knowledge) into the minds of individuals. Where group and social learning occurs, it is arguably built on the foundation of this set of assumptions; educational assessment, for instance, being uneasy at assigning marks and grades to groups, instead asks for an individualized account.

Though new digital technologies have the potential to disrupt these foundations, in reality they are currently often employed as a replacement for or augmentation of existing practices. The written word is replaced with the word processor, the textbook with the DVD or internet encyclopaedia, the overhead transparency with the whiteboard or PowerPoint presentation. At most, digital technologies are used to enhance and enrich these traditional practices – adding spellcheckers and font formatting, animations and videos. The fundamental pedagogic structure in relation to these technologies, along with the methods by which they mediate relationships with curriculum, is, however, left intact; the Cartesian model of learning remains undisrupted. More radical applications of new technologies – the use of Virtual Learning Environments (VLEs) to host podcasts and online texts and quizzes, for instance – tend to recreate offline structures and processes in an online medium. In essence, the ways of engaging and constructing knowledge and understanding established through the typographic revolution still pervade education and are thus mapped onto new digital technologies.

These technologies, however, facilitate – even necessitate – an entirely new method of engagement with knowledge and understanding, and it is possible to re-imagine educational practice in relation to this alternative approach. Applying the principles of Web 2.0, for instance, learners might be asked to construct their own wikis, drawing on information they discern for themselves. This is a process with a number of interesting pedagogical features. First, it derails the usual top-down curricular approach, in which learners are asked to assimilate a canon of sanctioned knowledge, and replaces it with a bottom-up model, in which learners actively identify and evaluate relevant information and useful understandings. This, in turn, disrupts authority and convention, opens education to multiple competing perspectives and ideas and begins to support learners in developing their capacities to evaluate both the relevance and validity of content – skills crucial to their future as digital citizens. Such an approach also erodes the boundaries between subject areas, which are no longer a necessary organizing principle of education. In exploring a topic such as genetically modified foods (GMOs), for instance, learners might draw together understandings from science, art and literature, geography, philosophy and religion and, in doing so, synthesize for themselves entirely new forms of understanding.

The second interesting feature of this use of technology is that it fosters collaboration between learners, collaboration which does not necessarily need to be geographically bounded. In doing so, it opens up additional perspectives and understandings of the world and supports a Vygotskian model of learning (see Chapter 1). The shift here would be away from a Cartesian, individualist model of learning in reference to a fixed, modernist canon of understanding towards a social, collaborative model, one which recognizes a pluralistic, postmodern universe of knowledge and the complexities of engagement within it.

Interestingly, this form of learning – and the types of radical impact that digital technologies might potentially have on educational provision and practices – echoes the work of Ivan Illich in the 1970s. In *Deschooling Society*, Illich accuses the current system of confusing means with outcomes; of conflating qualification and understanding, schooling and education, performance and learning. He calls for a reimagining of education, one which anticipates the potential offered by digital technologies.

> The current search for new educational funnels must be reversed into the search for their institutional inverse: educational webs which heighten the opportunity for each one to transform each moment of his living into one of learning, sharing, and caring. (Illich, 1973, vii)

The crucial call here is for a shift from the Cartesian model, in which the institution is most important, to a social, communal one, in which the autonomy and interest of the individual is most crucial, with institutions existing purely to be of service to them. Illich makes explicit reference to emerging computer technology (the mass reach of the internet was inconceivable to most at this point) to facilitate fluid, informal relationship between individuals for the sharing of expertise and experience – a not dissimilar situation to a social network such as Facebook. Detached from the institutional framing, relationships would be, not hierarchical, but cooperative and equal; the roles of teacher and student established momentarily rather than being fixed. For Illich, this deschooling of education should be taken to its literal extreme, so that education becomes something ongoing and central to people's lives rather than something contained within the school. Of course, Illich's proposals have never been taken to the heart of educational policy, as they would involve a shift too radical to be implemented. The rise of internet technologies have, however, created an alternative environment with the clear potential to realize his ideas; through Wikipedia and similar mediums, the notion of a peer-facilitated, fluid, interest-driven, ongoing web of learning can be envisaged.

Conclusions

The story given here of the relationship between knowledge and technology is also one in which power features fundamentally. In a key revolution, the implementation of a new technology disrupts existing ways of producing and consuming knowledge and understanding. These shifts have, in general, been broadly democratizing, widening access and allowing more and more perspectives to be heard. The extent of this process has, however, been repeatedly curtailed by the extent to which people are able to access that technology. In each revolution, particular groups within society, by nature of their ability to command these technologies, have been able to use them to their own ends, while others have been systematically disenfranchised.

In terms of the education system, it would seem naive to ignore these shifts in technology. If they are, as suggested here, capable of shaping and mediating society's knowledge system – and thus the basis of the curriculum – it would be remiss to discount them. The Cartesian, textbook-inspired system of education seems, in this respect, to stand at odds with wider shifts in the ways in which people are creating and consuming knowledge and understanding on the internet. Yet it would also be unwise to ignore the new patterns of power and privilege emerging through the digital divide, internet access and the capability of using these new technologies. There is a real risk that an educational system too reliant on these technologies might further disenfranchise those learners with no outside access. Still, it might be argued that for these individuals, an emersion in the use of online technologies within the school is even more important. Regardless of the answer, the reality outside is that young people – and learners more generally – will increasingly engage with online technology and that there will be informal educational processes underpinning this engagement, even if the formal system of schooling is unable to accommodate those processes.

Key questions

- How have historical technological revolutions impacted on the nature of society's knowledge and the ways that people distribute and interact with that knowledge?
- How have these shifts been framed by issues of power? How have they disrupted conventions of power?
- What is the significance of the more recent history of technology against this backdrop?
- How might the shape of the curriculum, as it currently exists, be partially understood as a product of the conventions of available technologies?
- Against this backdrop, what challenges do new technologies present? What opportunities do they offer in relation to curriculum and to educational practice and provision more widely?

Further reading

Eisenstein, E. (2005). *The Printing Press in Early Modern Europe*. Cambridge: Cambridge University Press.

Illich, I. (1973). *Deschooling Society*. London: Penguin.

McLuhan, M. (1962). *The Gutenberg Galaxy: The Making of Typographic Man*. Toronto: University of Toronto Press.

Pickover, C. (2010). 'The Rise of Internet Prosthetic Brains and Soliton Personhood'. Edge World Question Center, www.edge.org/q2010/q10_11.html (accessed 26 July 2010).

Seeley Brown, J., and R. Adler (2008). 'Minds on Fire: Open Education, the Long Tail and Learning 2.0'. *Educause Review*, http://net.educause.edu/ir/library/pdf/ERM0811.pdf.

School Ethos and the Role of Teachers

Chapter Outline

How does the day-to-day work within classrooms relate to the overall ethos of the school? What are the internal and external factors which influence the ethos, and how do they manifest themselves and influence the educational experience of the pupils? Who are the winners and losers of this ethos in schools? How do the previous chapters link into the development of ethos and in particular the external pressures schools are under from neoliberal ideologies of competition and choice? What follows is an overview of the main teaching styles, such as Grasha and Mosston, and how they link to the learning theories outlined in previous chapters.

Introduction

Parental choice of schools has been an integral part of educational policy, and the recent change of government does not suggest that change in the near future is likely. In fact, a recent White Paper, 'The Importance of Teaching', has suggested a strengthening of parental choice, including the option to form new schools in certain areas and under certain circumstances. What, though, do parents base their choice upon? In most instances the level of information available to parents is what they can gain from open days, league tables and OfSTED reports. The latter two are often criticized as not truly reflecting the nature of the school, the intake in terms of social factors (see Chapter 6) or the ethos and culture of the school. This, perhaps, is one of the most important aspects to consider in terms of choosing a school, but before we consider the creation and impact of culture and ethos, it is worth examining how and why school choice has become such a controversial issue within education.

Ideological positions and market forces

In order to fully understand the direction of policy design it is crucial to gain a sense of the political ideologies that policy creators adhere to. Arguably the main ideologies relevant to the political scene in the United Kingdom today are social democracy, neoliberalism and neoconservatism. A more detailed overview of these and other ideologies can be found in Fielding's (2001) book, *Taking Education Really Seriously: Four Years Hard Labour*, in addition to the chapters within this section.

Social democracy

Social democratic policies are characterized by aims of full employment, a strong welfare state and high taxes for high earners, which are distributed downwards through high-quality, well-resourced public services. Social democratic education policies tend to manifest support for a comprehensive educational system which allows access to all, has little or no selection by ability and expands educational availability by, for example, widening participation within higher education. Additionally, there is a commitment to ensuring equal opportunities for all, regardless of race, sex or socio-economic status, and to a largely unprescribed curriculum within schools, a curriculum which seeks to focus upon the individual needs of children to enable them to take part in a functional 'meritocratic' society.

Neoliberalism

Neoliberalist policies promote the involvement of private enterprise, in financial and structural terms, within public services. Furthermore, neoliberalist policies suggest that public services are best served by being opened up to general market forces; in particular, competition. In order to provide true competition, consumers – in the case of education, parents and children – need to be able to compare results, provided through the publication of league tables and OfSTED reports. Furthermore, for those results to have any meaning, education needs to be under strict control so that results can be compared on a like-for-like basis. This results in strict control of standards, teacher training and school performance. The publication of league tables necessitates frequent testing of pupils at various prescribed ages regardless of the individual child's readiness for any test. Neoliberalist policies suggest choice and freedom in education and allow for a range of schools, including academies and independent trust schools. However, because of the testing within schools and the subsequent publication of the results, schools are frequently less likely to offer truly alternative education (much as supermarkets are reluctant to differ greatly from each other) for fear of 'losing out' to the competition. For a more detailed discussion of neoliberalist policies, see Hill (2003).

Neoconservatism

Neoconservative and neoliberalist policies share some key philosophies in terms of high levels of control over schools; in fact, the former go further by enforcing a prescribed curriculum (the national curriculum) and pedagogy. The prescribed curriculum aims to ensure that neoconservatives' desire for a 'moral' education – including promotion of family values, respect for authority and heterosexual relationships – is at the foreground of content. The prescribed pedagogy suggests a homogeneous group of pupils who will benefit from similar teaching methods, most notably teacher-centred approaches. The promotion of Britishness and assimilation in regard to race, gender and class are given priority. In essence schools would be governed through strong state control.

Current system

The previous and current government in the United Kingdom certainly share some ideological positions, most notably the impact of market forces under a neoliberalist approach, which would promote the idea of school results forming a market in education within which parents could select their school. However, certain issues – the concept of Britishness and a move towards focusing on the basics of education, together with comments around discipline in school – would move more towards a neoconservative position (DfE 2010). This chapter is less concerned with the impact that the policies of market forces have upon education, although this is a serious issue, than with examining the culture of schools and their ability, together with teachers, to ensure that all children have an equal chance of succeeding. For more on the impact of testing, see Murphy, Mufti and Kassem (2008). In essence they argue that the position of schools in any league table is related more to the types of pupils they attract than to any great improvement within schools themselves.

School ethos

While OfSTED reports and league tables can show the levels of success that schools appear to achieve, they tell little of perhaps the most important aspects of education: the culture, or ethos, of the school and how likely a child is to fit into that ethos. Perhaps one of this book's most telling criticisms of the system is that it tends to promote a one-size-fits-all approach which does not truly reflect the increasingly diverse nature of our society. Attempts by some schools to do this met with strong opposition, as in the case of the William Tyndale School. It is necessary to consider whether parents are interested in a school's culture, whether schools do in fact have differing cultures and, of course, what school culture is and how it manifests itself. First, though, what the role of schools is must be considered, and how that role influences and directs culture assessed.

The role of schools

As discussed in Chapter 5, schools do not operate in a vacuum, free from the vagaries and influences of the wider society. In addition, they will come under pressure from economic needs, international comparisons and debates about good citizenship and socially acceptable behaviour. Therefore, increasingly schools must not only concern themselves with educational achievement but also consider how best to turn out well-rounded individuals who will become useful members of a wider society. Every Child Matters (2004) placed a responsibility on schools to focus on five key outcomes for children:

- be healthy
- stay safe
- enjoy and achieve
- make a positive contribution
- achieve economic well-being.

As can be seen, the only outcome one would immediately connect to the traditional role of schools would be the third one: enjoy and achieve. The rest are issues which schools have always been involved in but perhaps more in terms of how they relate to the likelihood of academic success than as a main aim.

So what do parents, the media, politicians and the rest of society expect from teachers and schools in this modern age? And is it present within the information we can access about our schools?

Defining culture

While the term 'culture' is frequently heard, read and used, it is an extremely problematic concept to define. Curtis and Pettigrew (2009) cite Williams (1983) as suggesting that 'it is one of the two or three most complicated words in the English language'. The reasons behind Williams's statement are clear: culture is a complicated concept in terms of getting agreement on its meaning from society as a whole. The diversity of English society is much commented upon; whether it is seen as a strength or weakness is often determined by ideological stance, but the fact that it is diverse is not in doubt. This diversity is based not only upon ethnicity but also upon class, location, age, sexual orientation and other issues. Therefore, while it would be politically and socially expedient to promote a culture which the entire society could work towards, realistically the suggestion of a dominant culture breaks down rather rapidly when it is subjected to any real and focused scrutiny. It is this multiplicity of cultures which makes the idea of a national school system a problematic one.

A culture can be seen as a shared set of understandings about how society operates and what its agreed **norms, values** and **beliefs** are. Norms can be expectations of behaviour and response to a given situation. Values underpin norms; one may speak of an underlying value of free speech or fairness. Beliefs can be seen as two-fold. First, there are uncontested beliefs, those concerning agreed and incontestable matters of fact; secondly, and of more relevance to this chapter, there are moral beliefs, which affect one's view of the world and the society in which one operates. (Curtis and Pettigrew 2009).

In terms of an overall societal culture, there is a further question: whether an attempt to create and maintain one that all can adhere to and agree upon is actually in the interests of all groups in society. Chapter 6 showed how certain groups are less likely to achieve than others, and one perspective is that those in positions of power deliberately seek to create such a situation, as it protects their position. Furthermore, the same group would then attempt to ensure that the current situation is not fundamentally challenged by ensuring that this state of affairs is seen as natural through the imposition of a national culture which assumes that certain groups are more likely to succeed than others.

A society may attempt to promote the idea of a national culture through a range of mediums which Althusser would class as ideological state apparatus. These mediums do not support culture through physical power but instead through promoting the imposed culture as one about which all agree and, furthermore, as one which benefits all. If certain groups seem to reap most of that benefit, that is simply the natural order of things; any challenge is a challenge to the overall way of life.

Therefore, building on Marx's and Engel's works, Althusser (1984) stated that there were two main forms of maintaining social control in an unjust society. First, there is what he termed the repressive state apparatus (RSA). Its elements – the army, the police force, the system of law and order – are rough tools; while they can, for short periods, maintain order, that order is likely to be challenged, as it is clear that individuals and groups within society are repressed. Think of dictatorships in numerous countries worldwide which are supported by the threat or reality of force from RSAs.

Far more subtle ways of control are those supported by the ideological state apparatus (ISA). Its tools are far more important, as the most effective way to ensure that there is no challenge to an unjust system is to convince the public that the system is just.

Althusser suggested that ISAs come in these forms:

- religious
- educational
- family
- legal
- political
- trade union
- communications
- cultural (literature, the arts, sports, etc.).

He stressed that one telling aspect of the ideological state apparatus was that many of them were privately owned or at least not under the direct control of the government (unlike repressive state apparatuses). A major indicator of how deeply hegemony has infiltrated the thinking of the population is when even institutions such as the trade unions, whose very role is to challenge, work within the system and in so doing become largely ineffective in achieving true change. As Althusser stated:

> no class can hold State power over a long period without at the same time exercising its hegemony over and in the State Ideological Apparatuses. (1984, 20)

Althusser's views can be linked to the move towards state control over the education system, as detailed within Chapter 5. They suggest a rather complicit approach to the imposed natural order by all aspects of the educational system, including schools, teachers and, most importantly, pupils. Later in this chapter, whether this is actually true or whether there is evidence that pupils challenge the system in a range of ways will be questioned.

School culture

While we have discussed how schools are not free to make their own decisions in terms of curriculum content and are held accountable in terms of achievement in relation to a range of standardized tests, it would be inaccurate and naive to suggest that all schools have the same culture or that the 'feel' of each school is the same. Therefore, while schools have certain responsibilities to adhere to, the way in which they approach them can differ. Schools are under a range of influences – these include, of course, national and local governance – but schools are also part of a community, and primary schools in particular must attempt to meet the local parents' conception of, as Metz (1991) described it, what a 'real school' is. What parents want and expect from a school, therefore, can differ from area to area. For example, educational success and high levels of academic achievement may be seen as more important than inclusion, diversity and a caring welfarist nature in certain areas – and just the opposite in others. Hargreaves (1995) suggested that there were two main domains in terms of culture. First, the instrumental domain, which relates to achievement and social order; secondly, the expressive domain, more concerned with relationships and socialization. He (in Stall, 2003, 99) envisages four types of school culture, depending on how much emphasis is placed on those domains:

- **traditional** – categorized by high academic standards, weak social cohesion between staff and students (with little time for those who do not perform academically) and fairly strict staff;
- **welfarist** – categorized by individual student development, relaxed and friendly atmosphere; academic goals are often a lower priority than social cohesion and respect (the 'caring' inner-city school is suggested as an example of this type of culture);
- **hothouse** – categorized by huge pressure to succeed (for both staff and students), with a frenetic pace; teachers are enthusiastic and expect the same of children; there is encouragement to join in, but it can be forced at times;
- **anomic** – categorized by a 'failing school' syndrome: little or no direction or team work, with underachieving students; to prevent misconduct, academic

work is not pushed; teachers, often feeling that there are low levels of support from above, suffer from insecurity and low morale.

With the expectation of the anomic school, it is not difficult to envisage scenarios within which schools in different communities would perhaps seek to create one culture in preference to another, depending on their understanding of the expectations of parents. Arguably one product of parental choice has been to ensure that schools reflect their catchment area, thus perpetuating the differences in educational achievement across various groups within society.

One can question how much autonomy schools, under the centralized system of education created by the Education Reform Act (1988), have had to truly take account of the needs of the pupils who attend them or whether accountability, in terms of league tables, ensured that the focus had to remain upon exam results. If schools are not in a position to reflect the communities they serve, it is more likely that the culture they promote will clash with that of pupils and parents, increasing the chances of low achievement and behavioural issues within schools. If schools are too centralized, in both their approaches and the ways in which levels of success are measured, then certain groups in society are more likely to fail.

Responsibility of schools and teachers

One telling influence upon school culture is the morale and status of teachers. To return to the earlier point about what is expected of teachers and schools, it is interesting to note that in recent years schools have been expected to provide out-of-school clubs at the start and end of the day, offer a range of extra-curricular activities and promote healthy eating and the benefits of exercise. This last area was brought most notably to attention by Jamie Oliver's campaign for healthier school dinners. This focus on schools as providers of social and physical development as much as educational development has accompanied increasing pressure being brought to bear on teachers and schools in other areas. Recent (2011) comments by Michael Gove have focused on school behaviour and on the responsibility and powers that teachers have to challenge that behaviour. His comments are worth discussing, as they suggest what could be classed as an alarming lack of awareness of what takes place within schools. His recent suggestions that teachers should have the capacity to confiscate mobile phones and even delete material they deem inappropriate from them seem destined to create many more problems than those they would alleviate. The idea that these approaches would not create significant conflict between teachers and pupils, not to mention parents, is at best naive. The further idea that teachers will have their anonymity protected when they are initially accused of inappropriate behaviour by a pupil appears just as problematic. First, it suggests that accusations of this nature are often false, potentially making pupils more reluctant to come forward. Secondly, it would be hard to offer anonymity, given that a teacher would presumably have to be suspended while an investigation took place.

The main thrust of these announcements concerns conflict between teachers and pupils. The idea that malicious accusations are the norm and that teachers and pupils are in constant conflict which require government intervention is a worrying direction for a minister of education to take. Perhaps a more considered approach, one looking to build commonality rather than focus upon the potential for conflict, would be more beneficial in the long term.

What makes a good teacher?

If we are examining ways in which teachers and pupils can work more closely together, then perhaps it is apt to consider what makes a good teacher. Chapter 5 discussed increased control over teacher training and the way in which prescribed pedagogy and content have increased within the educational system. In spite of this, there is a constant stream of rhetoric from both media and government suggesting that teachers need to improve and develop further. One ought to ask in what ways this could be achieved and whether increasing prescription is the most appropriate way to improve teaching or should teachers be allowed to take more responsibility for their actions and approaches and allowed to develop and adopt their own style and methods. Goldhaber (2002), in his review of the literature, suggests that measurable differences in teachers' qualifications, experience, level of subject knowledge, performance on vocabulary tests and pedagogical knowledge have little impact on what is considered a good teacher. In fact, Goldhaber suggests, these factors account for less than 3 per cent of the variables, with the remainder made up of more intangible factors: enthusiasm, humour, connection with pupils, skills at conveying knowledge, good relationships with parents and the like.

Further to this point, in January 2008 a Cambridge Assessment Research Seminar was held at the House of Commons to address the question 'What makes a good teacher?' There was general agreement that high levels of qualifications, subject knowledge and effective strategies were not sufficient. Instead teachers needed:

- to be allowed a level of autonomy in terms of identifying and adapting to their pupils' needs;
- to engage in a level of 'creative subversion' by adapting policy initiatives to suit the needs of their pupils;
- to promote active engagement in learning;
- to understand the relationship between themselves and the pupils;
- to reflect critically upon their own performance.

It is interesting to compare these findings to those in Chapter 5, which demonstrate that the new proposals by the ConDem government offer less opportunity for many of those suggestions, which require reflection and a deep understanding of theory, and instead move towards a practice-based approach largely within 'training schools' which, at first glance, would appear to offer significantly less opportunity to develop those skills and attributes.

In addition, the suggestion that trainee teachers must have a minimum of a 2:2 degree ('The Importance of Teaching' [2011]) does not reflect the findings of Goldhaber and the Cambridge Assessment Seminar; both stated that the level of qualifications held by a teacher was no guarantee of quality. The fact that fewer than 6 per cent of teachers who are accepted on a PGCE possess degrees below that level is another factor worth considering.

Teaching styles

Other chapters in this volume have discussed the learning styles of individuals and how they link to individual development of pupils. This idea, that each pupil has his or her own needs, is often discussed within education but arguably not fully reflected within policy. The other factor which needs to be considered and taken into account is teaching styles.

Stop, Think, Do

Think back to your favourite teachers. What made them favourites? Was it their skills and knowledge or things that were more intangible – their humour, empathy, personality?

Can good teachers be developed? If so, how?

Grasha (1996) suggested five broad styles of teaching. These styles are not to be considered absolutes, nor should they be regarded as definitive choices; rather, teachers should be aware of the approaches and 'borrow' from them according to their preference and what they perceive to be the needs of the children they teach. These styles, which will be replicated here, are useful to begin the approach questioning how teachers, or those who possess the ambition to become a teacher, can best develop their skills and techniques.

The expert

In this style the teacher is seen as an expert who displays detailed knowledge about his or her area. A transmission style of teaching, which is very much teacher focused, would largely be adopted. Students would be expected to learn and utilize information through the detailed input they receive as examples; anecdotes would be less likely to be used.

There are several advantages to this style of teaching:

- detailed information;
- a high level of knowledge;
- it challenges students to progress;
- the teacher has high status level.

Disadvantages of this teaching style are:

- that it can confuse certain students and leave them behind;
- that it can be intimidating;
- that the underpinnings of the skills or knowledge can be missed.

Formal authority

This is a rather formal approach to teaching which includes aspects of behaviour, learning goals and a clear structure and involves a clear focus upon expectations; traditional methods and lessons will usually be well structured and follow a similar pattern. In many ways this could be seen as the teaching style that is invoked when people hark back to the days of the three Rs [The three Rs refer to reading, writing and arithmetic and are commonly used as a shorthand for traditional methods and study and curriculum].

Advantages of this teaching style include:

- a clear structure;
- clear expectations;
- well-managed classrooms;
- consistency.

Disadvantages of this style of teaching are that

- it is a somewhat rigid approach;
- it will not suit all learners;
- it is not particularly flexible and can be restrictive;
- it can be difficult for less able students.

The delegator

In many ways this is similar to a role-model approach: the teacher develops an approach to learning and expects students to adhere to it. The teacher will direct students and demonstrate how to perform tasks or solve problems; students will observe and emulate the teacher and develop knowledge through their approaches.

Advantages of this style of teaching are that it:

- includes clear instructions;
- can give a positive model to emulate;
- helps with observation skills;
- provides a clear action to emulate.

Disadvantages of this teaching style are that:

- the method of the teacher may not be suitable for the student;
- students can feel inadequate if they fail to emulate techniques;

- it can be rigid and focused upon the teacher's methods, leading to a lack of discovery learning.

The facilitator

The teacher that adopts this style will often place an emphasis on personal relationships and offer questions, options and alternatives rather than present knowledge as an absolute. Since there will be an increased focus upon independent action and responsibility, the teacher should be both encouraging and challenging.

Advantages of this style are that it:

- is flexible in its approach;
- involves students in developing their own understanding;
- cultivates independence;
- potentially focuses on individual needs and goals;
- is supportive and encouraging.

The style's more negative aspects are that:

- it can be time consuming
- it can be intimidating for certain students
- at times a more direct approach may be more effective, particularly when certain facts need to be learned or a new topic is introduced;
- it can make certain students uncomfortable.

The delegator

Within this style teachers give students the opportunity to engage in independent and group work usually based around projects. The teacher will be there to offer support and guidance.

The advantages of this approach can be seen as:

- allowing students increased autonomy;
- catering for a range of learning approaches;
- allowing flexibility in learning;
- encouraging discovery learning (see Chapters 1 and 2).

Among its disadvantages are that it:

- can be difficult to manage;
- can disadvantage students who need more guidance.

The styles above would require teachers to be given the opportunities to reflect upon their approach, the learning theories of their pupils, the ethos and requirements of the school and the needs of any external examination system. Arguably the current system of education makes this difficult.

Critical pedagogy

Hill and Cole (2001) argue for an adoption of critical pedagogy within the school curriculum. This approach, as outlined by Giroux (1983), would move the curriculum away from the functional towards the critical. It would provide an insight into, for example, many of the theoretical concepts contained within this chapter. Furthermore, it would provide a critique of the system, allowing individuals to see both how they are influenced by the dominant cultures and how to address this need. It would seek to debate the class system and lay it open to critiques and inquiry. To adopt a critical pedagogy in schools would require a range of changes to be made. Currently, according to Giroux (1983) and others such as Apple (2004), schools and society give higher status to certain types of behaviour and, more crucially, knowledge. The promotion of high culture over low culture, for example, and the fact that the languages (Bernstein 1971) used at school do not correspond to those used in all homes within society can be said to disadvantage certain groups. However, critical pedagogy needs to go further than simply raise awareness of these issues; instead, it should actively seek to overcome them. Schools should respond to local needs, as opposed to a nationally set and standardized curriculum. Teachers should be aware of the culture of the community they serve and seek to link education to its needs. The education of the community should involve the community and should refer to local issues. Finally, teachers should instil hope with the language of possibility – something which, after an examination of the GCSE figures, is not possible within the current system. This is not to place the blame at the feet of individual teachers; rather, it suggests that within the current system teachers have little flexibility to effect changes.

Conclusion

It has become clear over recent years and successive governments that the role and responsibilities of schools has widened considerably. People increasingly look to schools and teachers to alleviate concerns which may be more properly the province of society as a whole. An examination of media stories concerning antisocial behaviour, obesity, poor diet and lack of exercise among UK children shows that blame is often placed at the door of schools, and government policy often supports this rhetoric in a variety of ways. It seems incongruous at times that while we often look to schools to challenge the failings of society, at the same time we appear to have little faith in teachers to create and maintain their own approaches to the development of pupils. It is apparent that the culture of a school and what makes a good teacher are related more to the individual needs of that school community than to a centrally prescribed approach and, furthermore, that high levels of qualifications alone do not necessarily impact strongly on the quality of any individual's or institution's teaching. While weaker teachers may benefit from strong prescription, care must be taken to ensure that this is not done at the expense of those teachers, the majority, who can choose the most appropriate style in a given circumstance. The call for schools and teachers to reflect more accurately the communities they serve is not a new one, but perhaps the time is now right to allow teachers to reclaim their professional status and for us – as governments, parents, students and society – to give them the flexibility to develop their own professional approach.

Key questions

- How did your parents choose your school, or how have you chosen schools for your own children? What did you base your choice upon?
- Which ideological position do you feel most accurately reflects the current government? Why?
- Are we expecting too much from schools and teachers? Examine the media for stories about young children; are they negative or positive?
- Which of Hargreaves's four cultures most accurately reflects your experience of school? Which one would you feel is the best to aim for?
- What makes a good teacher? Can you identify or develop one?

Further reading

Goldhaber, D. (2002). 'The Mystery of Good Teaching'. www.stcloudstate.edu/tpi/initiative/documents/preparation/The%20Mystery%20of%20Good%20Teaching.pdf.

—(2004). 'Can Teacher Quality Be Effectively Assessed?'. www.rinace.net/bliblio/Can%20teacher%20quality%20be%20effectively%20assessed.pdf.

Grasha, A. F. (1996). *Teaching with Style*. Pittsburgh: Alliance.

Stoll, L. (2003). 'School Culture and Improvement', in M. Preedy, R. Glatter and C. Wise (eds), *Strategic Leadership and Educational Improvement*. Milton Keynes: Oxford University Press.

Tomlinson, S. (2005). *Education in a Post-Welfare Society*, 2nd edn. Milton Keynes: Oxford University Press.

Conclusion

Throughout this volume issues relating to teaching, learning, state control over the curriculum and the ways in which individuals and groups can resist that state of affairs have been examined. Technological advances and how they may impact upon the educational experience of individuals have also been examined.

The fast-moving nature of technology often parallels changes in educational policy, which successive governments and ministers for education develop, tinker with and change. At the time of writing, we are in one of those periods of change, as Michael Gove, the minster for education under the coalition government, presses ahead with his own agenda for changes to the educational system. The centralizing of control over the educational system has been previously discussed, and it is right for all those involved in education to challenge this concept and to critique and question the details within it.

Challenging policy

Dave Hill (2006) suggests that there are questions to be asked of any policy. He lists these as aims, contexts and impacts; he asks for consideration of the stated aims of every policy, from the point of view of both its creators and its detractors, and of its likely effects. Hill further suggests that questioners place the policy in context: what are the overall plans of the government in power, and how does the policy fit into their ideology? Finally, Hill asks for consideration of the consequences of the policy: who will win and who will lose? More specifically, which gender, race and class groups may win or lose? (Hill, 2006, 73).

New government plans

These questions are valid ones, and it is worth considering them in relation to the policy direction of the coalition government of 2011. Towards the end of 2010, the coalition published their White Paper on education, 'The Importance of Teaching', together with a supporting document entitled 'The Case for Change', which attempts to outline the need for a new educational policy.

'The Case for Change' suggests that England is falling behind some of its international competitors in the latest round of international testing of 15-year-olds through PISA; furthermore, that the impact of social class (see earlier chapters) on educational performance is greater in England than in Finland, for example. The document suggests that

> England had one of the highest gaps between high and low performing pupils and a strong relationship between social background and performance. 13.9 per cent of the variance in performance of pupils in England could be explained by their social background, as compared to just 8.3% in Finland and 8.2% in Canada. (3)

The importance of international competiveness and of attempting to ensure that achievement across all groups is raised is primarily related to the changing nature of the UK economy and the types of jobs available. As unskilled and low-skilled jobs are either replaced through technological advances or, more commonly, moved to other countries where they can be done more cheaply, the jobs that remain in England and the rest of the United Kingdom require higher qualification levels – hence, the need to improve education and the levels of success within it. Additionally, the types of industries which offer these new types of jobs have no particular requirement to be based in a specific country. A consequence of global communications is that the country where the idea for, say, a new mobile phone is developed or even where the actual product is created is not important. Companies will thus locate their offices and development labs in countries with good levels of educational achievement in science and technology and other areas that they need. Obviously issues such as employment laws and tax status play a major role here as well, but education is an important factor.

Here we can see that we are meeting Hill's first area to question that of the aims of the policy. We can question it in terms of why it has been created and secondly start to examine the way in which the policy relates to its wider context both within education and society.

How then does this policy relate to the achievement of its ambitions? While it would be difficult to argue that reducing educational inequalities based on social class and striving to make England's education system internationally respected are not worthwhile aims, we must question whether the proposed changes are likely to achieve them.

Their first idea is to create and support more good teachers. 'The Case for Change' states, 'Pupil progress depends more on the quality of teaching than anything else' (6). This type of statement should immediately put a critical reader on guard, in that, while a case can be made for this statement, the evidence to suggest this is not beyond dispute and furthermore, if we agreed with this statement then are we suggesting that the level of teaching across schools in challenging areas is significantly worse than that in other schools? This type of approach, examining teaching, draws us away from arguments about inequalities within the system and how they can be best challenged. The complexity of determining what makes a good teacher was discussed earlier in this volume; the government tend to link it to qualifications and to attracting more teachers from the top universities. Yet it is highly debatable whether 'good' teaching is linked to qualifications; research by Goldhaber (2002) claims that an overall review of the literature suggests that this is not the case. Currently fewer than 6 per cent of teachers have less than a 2:1 degree classification; thus, teaching is attracting the higher-level graduates already.

Linked to this debate is how teachers are actually trained. At the time of writing, the details of the proposed changes to teacher training are somewhat vague, but they will certainly include more practice in the classroom and more of the training being done in schools rather than universities. This suggests that teaching is a practical activity rather than a critical, reflective one. 'The Case for Change' suggests that some students felt their teacher training was too theoretical, although by no means was this a majority view. Furthermore, the importance of the theoretical underpinnings of practice are not always immediately apparent to new teachers as they settle into their first jobs, but they do give teachers the opportunity to grow and develop as they gain more experience. It is highly debatable that increased practice will improve teaching, and we wait with interest to see how this policy manifests itself.

One interesting area within 'The Case for Change' is the idea for less prescription of teaching methods to allow teachers to develop their own strategies for pushing pupils to the next level. As was earlier stated, this would be, on its face at least, a retreat from the state intervention that followed Callaghan's Ruskin Speech and the 1988 Educational Reform Act. It is somewhat confusing, though, to suggest that we allow teachers more autonomy while at the same time removing much of their training which supports a critical examination of theory and reflection. How can teachers be expected to understand their role fully and navigate their way through theories and practice to develop the best approach? If too much focus is on practical aspects, is it not less likely that teachers will challenge their own roles and approaches in order to improve?

In many ways linked to this issue of less prescription is the idea of free schools – those having freedom from local authority control and increased powers to change the curriculum, increase the focus on discipline, change teacher's pay structure and extend school hours; these are, effectively, quite wide-ranging powers. The schools can theoretically be set up by parent groups, businesses and charitable bodies, among others. The challenge here is to link to the issue of reducing educational inequality based on social class. While free schools and the like could have the opportunity to reflect local needs far more effectively, it is crucial to keep a close and critical eye on the organizations setting up the schools and the aims they have. There have already been suggestions that the schools will guarantee places to children whose parents have been involved in their creation – a way, critics suggest, of reducing the protection that the current open-admissions policy provides. Mary Bousted, the general secretary of the Association of Teachers and Lecturers, stated, 'It completely paves the way for pushy, middle-class parents to set up a school so their children don't have to go to the same school as the great unwashed. It makes a mockery of the idea that free schools are for all. They are not for everybody – we know they are disproportionately in the less deprived communities, where these schools are not needed' ('Row over free school admission plan', *The Independent*, 11 March 2011).

The true test of the free schools will be in how effective they are in increasing attainment across all social groups. Current criticism of their progress suggests that they may well have the opposite effect. At the time of writing, most of the applications have not come from areas where there is poor school provision – which gives further credence to Mary Bousted's criticisms.

One of the largest proposed changes is the introduction of the English baccalaureate, which includes English, maths, science, a language and history or geography. It is designed to push these subjects within schools and hold them accountable for the number of pupils who reach the required level in those subjects. The narrowing of the curriculum and the value judgements about what are the most important areas to study are not unproblematic. First, how does these goals relate to suggestions of increased autonomy and flexibility within the curriculum? Is it right to suggest that schools can respond to local needs effectively when they are constrained in terms of what is considered acceptable achievement? The focus on academic subjects has the potential to stigmatize and demotivate pupils whose abilities do not lie within academic study. There is no doubt that schools will need to promote and focus on these subjects, potentially at the expense of other areas of the curriculum. It does give an indication that the rhetoric of freedom, flexibility and autonomy is likely to remain just that – rhetoric – and be less likely to achieve the hoped-for changes and levels of success.

Throughout, this volume has presented a critical examination of issues related to teaching. learning and the curriculum. While many of these are school related, it is important to note that factors outside school have as much impact and arguably more on the levels of educational success that individuals and groups achieve. The impact of families, local communities, wealth and social-class inequalities all play a major role in determining achievement or its absence. That is not to say that schools and teachers are not of crucial importance. When we seek to educate, we surely seek to invoke curiosity, challenge and criticality If we wish to develop these skills within pupils, then we must ensure we adhere to them ourselves as teachers or students of education. Criticality is not the same as criticism; instead, it asks us to challenge and question suggested approaches, be they from government, theoretical perspectives, tutors or media interests. While theory and reflection may not provide all the answers, they do offer alternatives; to improve the educational system as a whole – or what is more likely, improve our approach within it – this knowledge is crucial.

The chapters in this book are designed, not to tell teachers and future educators how to teach, but to give them scope to create and develop their own approaches based on the best available evidence and the context in which they find themselves. It is through this approach that we believe education, and the experiences individuals have within it, will improve – not through prescription, direction and an overfocus on qualifications.

References

Abbot, D. (2005). 'Teachers Are Failing Black Boys', in B. Richardson (ed.), *Tell It Like It Is: How Our Schools Fail Black Children*. London: Bookmarks.

Alexander, R. (2001). *Culture and Pedagogy: International Comparisons in Primary Education*. Oxford: Blackwell.

—(2008a). *Essays on Pedagogy*. Abingdon: Routledge.

—(2008b). *Towards Dialogic Teaching: Rethinking Classroom Talk*. York: Dialogos.

—(ed.) (2009). *Children, Their World, Their Education: Final Report and Recommendations of the Cambridge Primary Review*. London: Routledge.

Ally, M. (2008). 'Foundations of Educational Theory for Online Learning', in T. Anderson (ed.), *The Theory and Practice of Online Learning*. Edmonton: Athabasca University Press.

Apple, M. (2003). *The State and Politics of Knowledge*. New York: Routledge.

Aristotle. (2000). *Politics*. Trans. Ernest Barker. London: Pearson Education.

Ausubel, D. (1963). *The Psychology of Meaningful Verbal Learning*. New York: Grune & Stratton.

—(1968). *Educational Psychology, A Cognitive View*. Austin, TX: Holt, Rinehart and Winston.

—(1969). *School Learning*. Austin, TX: Holt, Rinehart and Winston.

Bakhtin, M. (1982). *The Dialogic Imagination: Four Essays*. Austin: University of Texas Press.

Bandura, A. (1973). *Aggression: A Social Learning Analysis*. Englewood Cliffs, NJ: Prentice-Hall.

—(1977). *Social Learning Theory*. Englewood Cliffs, NJ: Prentice Hall.

Bates, J., and S. Lewis (2009). *The Study of Education: An Introduction*. Continuum: London.

Bernstein, B. (1971). *Class, Codes and Control*. London: Paladin.

Biggs, J. (1999). *Teaching for Quality Learning at University*. Buckingham: Open University Press.

Binet, A., and T. Simon (1916). *The Development of Intelligence in Children*. Baltimore: Williams and Wilkins.

Bobbitt, F. (1918). *The Curriculum*. Boston: Houghton Mifflin.

Bourdieu, P., and J. Passeron (1973). 'Cultural Reproduction and Social Reproduction', in B. Richard (ed.), *Knowledge, Education and Cultural Change*. London: Tavistock.

Bowles, S., and H. Gintis (1976). *Schooling in Capitalist America: Educational Reform and the Contradictions of Economic Life*. London: Routledge and Kegan Paul.

—(2001). *Schooling in Capitalist America: Revisited*. e\papers\JEP-paper\sociology of education.tex.

Brown, Seely, J., and R. Adler (2008). 'Minds on Fire: Open Education, the Long Tail and Learning 2.0'. http://net.educause.edu/ir/library/pdf/ERM0811.pdf (accessed 27 July 2010).

Brown, A., J. Bransford, R. Ferrara and J. Campione (1983). 'Learning, Remembering and Understanding', in P. Mussen (ed.), *Handbook of Child Psychology*. New York: John Wiley.

Bruner, J. (1960). *The Process of Education*. Cambridge, MA: Harvard University Press.

—(1961). 'The act of discovery'. *Harvard Educational Review*, 31, 21–32.

—(1966). *Toward a Theory of Instruction*. Cambridge, MA: Harvard University Press.

—(1986). *Actual Minds, Possible Worlds*. Cambridge, MA: Harvard University Press.

—(1990). *Acts of Meaning*. Cambridge, MA: Harvard University Press.

Coffield, F., D. Moseley, E. Hall and K. Ecclestone (2004). *Learning Styles and Pedagogy in Post-16 Learning. A Systematic and Critical Review*. London: Learning and Skills Research Centre.

Coffin, C., and K. O'Halloran (2008). 'Researching argumentation in educational contexts: New directions, new methods'. *International Journal of Research and Method in Education*, 31 (3), 219–27.

Cox, C., and A. Dyson (eds) (1971). *The Black Papers on Education*. London: Davis-Poynter.

Curry, L. (1983). 'An Organization of Learning Styles Theories and Constructs'. Paper presented at the Annual Meeting of the American Educational Research Association, Montreal, PQ.

Dalrymple, D. (2010). 'Knowledge Is Out, Focus Is In, and People Are Everywhere'. www.edge.org/q2010/q10_16.html#dalrymple (accessed 26 July 2010).

Dawes, L., N. Mercer and R. Wegerif (2000). *Thinking Together: A Programme of Activities for Developing Thinking Skills at KS2*. Birmingham: Questions Publishing.

DCSF. (2008). *The Assessment for Learning Strategy*. London: Crown.

Deleuze, G., and F. Guattari (1980). *A Thousand Plateaus*. London: Continuum.

Dewey, J. (1938). *Experience and Education*. New York: Macmillan.

DfE (2010). 'The Case for Change'.

DfE (2010). The Importance of Teaching.

Dove, A. (1971). 'The "Chitling" Test', in L. Aiken (ed.), *Psychological and Educational Testings*. Boston: Allyn and Bacon.

Dunn, R. (2000). 'Learning styles: Theory, research and practice'. *National Forum of Applied Educational Research Journal*, 13 (1), 3–22.

Durkheim, E. (2008). *The Elementary Forms of Religious Life*. Oxford: Oxford Paperbacks.

Edwards, D., and N. Mercer (1987). *Common Knowledge: The Development of Understanding in the Classroom*. London: Falmer Press.

Eisenstein, E. (2005). *The Printing Press in Early Modern Europe*. Cambridge: Cambridge University Press.

Evans, G. (2006). *Educational Failure and White Working Class Children in Britain*. Hampshire: Palgrave MacMillan.

Fielding, M. (2001). *Taking Education Really Seriously: Four Years Hard Labour*. New York: Routledge Falmer.

Flavell, J. (1979). 'Metacognition and cognitive monitoring: A new area of cognitive-developmental inquiry'. *American Psychologist*, 34, 906–11.

—(1987). 'Speculations About the Nature and Development of Metacognition', in F. Weinert and R. Kluwe (eds), *Metacognition, Motivation and Understanding*. Hillsdale, NJ: Erlbaum, 21–9.

Fleming, N. (2001). VARK – 'A Guide to Learning Styles'. www.vark-learn.com/english/index.asp (accessed 17 June 2010).

Foucault, M. (1969). *The Archaeology of Knowledge*. London: Routledge.

—(1979). *The History of Sexuality: Volume 1*. Harmondsworth: Penguin.

—(2001). *The Order of Things: Archaeology of the Human Sciences*. London: Routledge.

Freire, P. (1996). *Pedagogy of the Oppressed* (rev. edn). London: Penguin.

—(2001). *Pedagogy of Freedom: Ethics, Democracy and Civic Courage*. New York: Rowman and Littlefield.

Gagné, R. (1977). *Conditions of Learning*. Andover, MA: Thomson Learning.

Galton, F. (1869). 'Hereditary Genius: An Inquiry into Its Laws and Consequences'. http://tinyurl.com/galton1 (Google Books database).

—(1883). *Inquiries into the Human Faculty and Its Development*. http://galton.org/books/human-faculty/text/galton-1883-human-faculty-v4.pdf.

Gardner, H. (1983). *Frames of Mind: The Theory of Multiple Intelligences*. New York: Basic Books.

—(1993). *Multiple Intelligences: The Theory in Practice*. New York: Basic Books.

Gibb, N. (2010). Speech given to the Reform Conference. www.education.gov.uk/news/speeches/ng-reform-conference (accessed 26 July 2010).

Giles, J. (2005). 'Internet encyclopaedias go head to head'. *Nature*, 483 (1), 900–1.

Giroux, H. (2001). *Theory and Resistance in Education: Towards a Pedagogy for the Opposition*. Westport, CT: Greenwood Press.

Goldhaber, D. (2002). 'The Mystery of Good Teaching'. www.educationnext.org/20021/.50.html.

Gould, S. (1982). 'A nation of morons'. *New Scientist*, (6 May), 349–52.

—(1996). *The Mismeasure of Man*. New York: Norton.

Gramsci, A. (1929–35). *Selections from the Prison Notebook*. London: Lawrence and Wishart.

Grasha, A. F. (1996). *Teaching with Style*. Pittsburgh: Alliance Publishers.

Greene, D., B. Sternberg and M. Lepper (1976). 'Overjustification in a token economy'. *Journal of Personality and Social Psychology*, 34, 1219–34.

Guilford, J. (1967). *The Nature of Human Intelligence*. New York: McGraw-Hill.

Harris, B. (1979). 'Whatever happened to Little Albert?' *American Psychologist*, 34 (2), 151–60.

Hatcher, R. (2001). 'Getting down to business: Schooling in the globalised economy'. *Education and Social Justice*, 3 (2), 45–9.

—(2004). 'Social Class and School', in D. Matheson (ed.), *An Introduction to the Study of Education*, 3rd edn. London: RouteledgeFalmer.

Herrnstein, R., and C. Murray (1996). *The Bell Curve: Intelligence and Class Structure in American Life*. London: Simon and Schuster.

Hill, D., and M. Cole (2004). *Schooling and Equality: Fact, Concept and Policy*. London: Routledge.

Hirst, P., and R. Peters (1970). *The Logic of Education*. London: Routledge and Kegan Paul.

Hutchins, E. (1995). *Cognition in the Wild*. Cambridge, MA: MIT Press.

Illich, I. (1973). *Deschooling Society*. London: Penguin.

Internet World Stats (2010). Internet usage statistics. www.internetworldstats.com/stats.htm (accessed 27 July 2010).

Joseph, G. G. (2000). *The Crest of the Peacock: Non-European Roots of Mathematics*. London: Penguin.

Kant, I. (2007). *Critique of Pure Reason*. London: Penguin Modern Classics.

Kelly, A. V. (2004). *The Curriculum: Theory and Practice*, 5th edn. London: Sage Publications.

Kerr, B. (2007). 'Which Radical Discontinuity?' http://billkerr2.blogspot.com/2007/02/which-radical-discontinuity.html (accessed 25 August 2010).

Klein, P. (1997). 'Multiplying the problems of intelligence by eight: A critique of Gardner's theory'. *Canadian Journal of Education*, 22 (4), 377–94.

Kolb, D. (1984). *Experiential Learning*. Englewood Cliffs, NJ: Prentice Hall.

Lave, J., and E. Wenger (1991). *Situated Learning: Legitimate Peripheral Participation*. Cambridge, MA: Cambridge University Press.

—(1998). *Communities of Practice: Learning, Meaning and Identity*. Cambridge, MA: Cambridge University Press.

Lepper, M. R., D. Greene and R. E. Nisbett (1973). 'Undermining children's intrinsic interest with extrinsic reward: A test of the "overjustification" hypothesis'. *Journal of Personality and Social Psychology*, 28, 129–37.

Lévi-Strauss, C. (2001). *Myth and Meaning*. London: Routledge.

Malinowski, B. (1978). *Argonauts of the Western Pacific*. London: Routledge.

Marsh, J., and E. Millard (2000). *Literacy and Popular Culture: Using Children's Culture in the Classroom*. London: Sage Publications.

Martin, J. (2004). 'Gender in Education', in D. Matheson (ed.), *An Introduction to the Study of Education*, 3rd edn. London: RouteledgeFalmer.

McCarthy, B. (1980). *The 4MAT System: Teaching to Learning Styles with Right/Left Mode Techniques*. Barrington, IL: Excel.

McDonald, A., and P. Newton (2001). *A Pilot of Aptitude Testing for University Entrants*. Slough: NfER.

McLuhan, M. (1962). *The Guttenberg Galaxy: The Making of Typographic Man*. Toronto: University of Toronto Press.

—(1964). *Understanding Media: The Extensions of Man*. New York: McGraw-Hill.

—(1967). *The Medium Is the Message: An Inventory of Effects*. New York: Random House.

Mercer, N. (1995). *The Guided Construction of Knowledge: Talk Amongst Teachers and Learners*. Clevedon: Multilingual Matters.

—(2000). *Words and Minds*. London: Routledge.

Miller, N., and J. Dollard (1941). *Social Learning and Imitation*. London: Yale University Press.

Mount, F. (2010). *'Mind the Gap': The New Class Divide in Britain*. Croydon: Bookmarque.

Murphy, L., E. Mufti and D. Kassem (2008). *Education Studies: An Introduction.*

Myers, I. (1962). *The Myers-Briggs Type Indicator.* Palo Alto, CA: Consulting Psychologists Press.

Pavlov, I. (1927). *Conditioned Reflexes.* London: Routledge and Kegan Paul.

Perry, E. and Francis, B. (2008). *The Social Class Gap For Educational Achievement: A Review Of The Literature.* www.thersa.org/__data/assets/pdf_file/0019/367003/RSA-Social-Justice-paper.pdf

Piaget, J. (1971). *Biology and Knowledge.* Chicago: University of Chicago Press.

—(1985). *The Equilibration of Cognitive Structures: The Central Problem of Intellectual Development.* Chicago: University of Chicago Press.

Pickover, C. (2010). 'The Rise of Internet Prosthetic Brains and Soliton Personhood'. www.edge.org/q2010/q10_11.html (accessed 26 July 2010).

Plato (2007). *The Republic.* Trans. H. D. P. Lee. London: Penguin Classics.

Plowden, B. (1967). *Children and Their Primary Schools: Report of the Central Advisory Council for Education (England).* London: HMSO.

Pollard, M. (2009). *Internet Access: Households and Individuals.* London: Crown.

Reigeluth, C. (1987). 'Lesson Blueprints Based Upon the Elaboration Theory of Instruction', in C. Reigeluth (ed.), *Instructional Design Theories in Action.* Hillsdale, NJ: Erlbaum Associates.

—(1992). 'Elaborating the elaboration theory'. *Educational Technology, Research and Development,* 40 (3), 80–6.

Robin, F. (1970). *Effective Study.* New York: Harper and Row.

Rose, J. (2009). *Independent Review of the Primary Curriculum: Final Report.* London: Crown Publications.

Rotter, J. B. (1945). *Social Learning and Clinical Psychology.* Englewood Cliffs, NJ: Prentice-Hall.

Rushton, J., and A. Jensen (2005). 'Thirty years of research into race differences and cognitive ability'. *Psychology, Public Policy and Law,* 11 (2), 235–94.

Salomon, G. (1993). *Distributed Cognitions: Psychological and Educational Considerations.* Cambridge, MA: Cambridge University Press.

Schilling, M. (1986). 'Knowledge and liberal education: A critique of Paul Hirst'. *Journal of Curriculum Studies,* 18 (1), 1–16.

Seligman, M. E. P., and S. F. Maier (1967). 'Failure to escape traumatic shock'. *Journal of Experimental Psychology,* 74, 1–9.

Sewell, T. (1997). *Black Masculinities and Schooling.* Stoke-on-Trent: Trentham Books.

Shlain, L. (1999). *The Alphabet Versus the Goddess.* London: Penguin.

Siemens, G. (2005). 'Connectivism: A learning theory for the digital age'. *International Journal of Instructional Technology and Distance Learning,* 2 (10). www.itdl.org/Journal/Jan_05/article01.htm.

Skinner, B. F. (1938). *The Behavior of Organisms: An Experimental Analysis.* Cambridge, MA: B. F. Skinner Foundation.

—(1947). '"Superstition" in the pigeon'. *Journal of Experimental Psychology,* 38.

—(1953). *Science and Human Behaviour.* www.bfskinner.org/BFSkinner/PDFBooks.html.

—(1957). *Verbal Behaviour.* Acton, MA: Copley Publishing Group.

—(1958). *The Technology of Teaching.* New York: Appleton-Century-Crofts.

—(1969). *Contingencies of Reinforcement.* New York: Appleton-Century-Crofts.

—(1988). *About Behaviourism*. New York: Random House.

Skinner, B., and C. B. Ferster (1957). *Schedules of Reinforcement*. New York: Appleton-Century-Crofts.

Spearman, C. (1927). *The Abilities of Man*. London: MacMillan.

Sperry, R. (1968). 'Hemisphere deconnection and unity in consciousness'. *American Psychologist*, 23, 723–33.

Stenhouse, L. (1975). *An Introduction to Curriculum Research and Development*. London: Heineman.

Stern, W. (1914). *The Psychological Methods of Intelligence Testing*. Baltimore: Warwick.

Taylor, F. W. (1911). *Principles of Scientific Management*. New York: Harper and Brothers.

Tennant, M. (1997). *Psychology and Adult Learning*. London: Routledge.

—(1916). *The Measurement of Intelligence*. Rolling Meadows, Illinois: Riverside Press.

Thorndike, E. L. (1911). *Animal Intelligence*. London: MacMillan.

Thurstone, L. (1924). *The Nature of Intelligence*. London: Routledge.

Tomlinson, M. (2004). *Final Report of the Working Group on 14-19 Reform*. London: Crown. www.dcsf.gov.uk/14-19/documents/Final%20Report.pdf.

—(2005) *Education in a Post-Welfare Society*, 2nd edn. Milton Keynes: Oxford University Press.

Topping, K., and S. Wolfendale. (1985). *Parental Involvement in Children's Reading*. New York: Nichols.

Tyler, R. (1949). *Basic Principles of Curriculum and Instruction*. Chicago: University of Chicago Press.

Verhagen, P. (2006). 'Connectivism: A New Learning Theory?' www.surfspace.nl/nl/Redactie-omgeving/Publicaties/Documents/Connectivism%20a%20new%20theory.pdf (accessed 25 August 2010).

Vernon, P. (1950). *The Structure of Human Abilities*. London: Methuen.

Vitale, B. (1985). *Unicorns Are Real: A Right-Brain Approach to Learning*. Austin, TX: Jalmar Press.

Vygotsky, L. (1978). *Mind in Society: The Development of Higher Psychological Processes*. Cambridge, MA: Harvard University Press.

—(1987). *Thought and Language*. Cambridge, MA: MIT Press.

Warnock, M. (1977). *Schools of Thought*. London: Faber.

Watson, J. (1914). *Behavior: A Textbook of Comparative Psychology*. New York: Henry Holt.

Watson, J., and R. Rayner (1920). 'Conditioned emotional reactions'. *Journal of Experimental Psychology*, 3 (1), 1–14.

Wechsler, D. (1949). *The Wechsler Intelligence Scale for Children*. New York: Psychological Corp.

Williams, R. L. (1972). 'The BITCH-100: A Culture-Specific Test'. Paper presented at the American Psychological Association Annual Convention, Honolulu.

Willis, P. (1977). *Learning to Labour*. Farnborough: Saxon House.

Wood, D., J. Bruner and G. Ross (1976). 'The role of tutoring in problem solving'. *Journal of Child Psychology and Psychiatry*, 17, 89–100.

Yerkes, R. (1914). *Psychological Examining in the United States Army*. Washington, DC: U.S. Surgeon General's Office.

Index